⌻B The Practitioner's Bookshelf

Hands-On Literacy Books for
Classroom Teachers and Administrators

Dorothy S. Strickland
FOUNDING EDITOR, LANGUAGE AND LITERACY SERIES

Celia Genishi and Donna E. Alvermann
LANGUAGE AND LITERACY SERIES EDITORS*

---

* For a list of current titles in the Language and Literacy Series, see *www.tcpress.com*

Bring It to Class
Unpacking Pop Culture in Literacy Learning

MARGARET C. HAGOOD
DONNA E. ALVERMANN
ALISON HERON-HRUBY

Foreword by Kylene Beers

TEACHERS COLLEGE PRESS Teachers College, Columbia University
New York and London

Published by Teachers College Press, 1234 Amsterdam Avenue, New York, NY 10027

Library of Congress Cataloging-in-Publication Data

Hagood, Margaret C.
    Bring it to class : unpacking pop culture in literacy learning / Margaret C. Hagood, Donna E. Alvermann, Alison Heron-Hruby ; foreword by Kylene Beers.
        p. cm. — (The practitioner's bookshelf)
    Includes bibliographical references and index.
    ISBN 978-0-8077-5061-2 (pbk. : alk. paper)
    1. Education—Sociological aspects—United States. 2. Language arts—United States. 3. Popular culture—United States. I. Alvermann, Donna E. II. Heron-Hruby, Alison. III. Title.
LC191.H22 2010
428.0071—dc22   2009043076

ISBN 978-0-8077-5061-2 (paper)

Printed on acid-free paper
Manufactured in the United States of America

17   16   15   14   13   12   11   10   8   7   6   5   4   3   2   1

Contents

Foreword

While at the 2008 National Council of Teachers of English (NCTE) convention, I answered an AP English teacher honestly when she asked me what I had read during the previous month. I don't remember all the books I listed, but I do remember one, not because of the book but because of her response. After I mentioned one of the *Harry Potter* novels, she interrupted me and said she was surprised to hear I wasted my time on such "popular fiction" when there were so many great classics to be enjoyed, "such as *War and Peace*." Before I could offer a response, she continued her lecture on the value of "real" literature and how popular literature could only be seen as a stepping stone to "better" books. To her, popular literature—"*Da Vinci Code* books"—appeal to the less-educated because they demand so little. She called young adult literature and popular adult fiction "drive-by books" because, as she explained, readers ought to drive by them on their way to the classics. Finally, reading my face, she stopped mid-sentence. After a brief moment of silence she said, "Well, perhaps because you've never taught AP English, you don't really understand the great literature students are capable of reading. Perhaps the students *you* work with really ought to stick to pop culture. Perhaps that's all they can read." And then she left.

While I was disappointed at her abrupt departure, I wasn't surprised at her attitude. In too many places and too many times, popular culture texts are seen as "easy reads," "fads," or "teen reading," or even "inappropriate" texts—whether print, film, or music. In 2007, at a state English/language arts convention, when I asked the audience of about 500 secondary teachers to define popular culture texts, the most common response was, "What the mainstream media provides." Most of the teachers agreed that, "It's what kids read outside of school but isn't appropriate for school." When asked why it's not appropriate for school, the answers were equally divided: "Pop culture is easy, so kids don't need help understanding it"; "Pop culture is what's popular for the moment, so there's no reason to study something that will change so quickly"; and "Pop culture contains language and images that are not appropriate for school-based discussions." Though some teachers did point out that rap was being used more often as a part of poetry discussions, most said that kids "got" rap without instruction so there was no reason to spend valuable instructional time discussing this genre. Another group pointed out that for reluctant readers, pop culture texts offer "a way in," but these teachers, as the one who lectured me earlier, also stated that these texts are still best used as springboards to "real" literature.

*   *   *

I wish I knew then what I know now, after reading *Bring It to Class: Unpacking Pop Culture in Literacy Learning*. I wish that back in 2007 and 2008 I had understood the concept of turn-around pedagogies and the literacy of fusion. I wish the three authors of this book had already handed this text to me so that I would have been better equipped to talk about how 21st-century demands, today's "anytime, anywhere" learners, multimodal texts, standards, and home and school literacy practices all intersect, creating nothing less than an educational mashup that clearly reveals the value of using texts that connect—pop culture texts, school texts, and student-created texts. I wish I could share with the AP English teacher at the 2007 NCTE convention and the secondary teachers at the 2008 convention many of the activities offered in *Bring It to Class* because *all* students—not just the ones who struggle to read, but all students—will benefit from the critical, evaluative, collaborative, and creative thinking activities in this book.

Margaret Hagood, Donna Alvermann, and Alison Heron-Hruby go beyond offering some ways to bring popular culture texts into a classroom. They challenge our understanding of what it means to read, of what defines something as a text, of what it means to construct meaning—of what culture *is*. They remind us that in today's world, "attention—not information—is in scarce supply," a sentence

that caught me up short and became my cornerstone for constructing meaning throughout the rest of the book. If I agree—and I do—that attention is what is in scarce supply, then I would be smart to wonder how popular culture texts, which already have students' attention, can be a part of the curriculum. The authors would argue, how can it *not*?

* * *

Recently, Thomas Friedman (2006) announced that the world is flat once again. "In the future," he said, "*how* we educate our children may prove to be more important than *how much* we educate them" (p. 301). He is reminding us of a principle that may have faded into the background as we have been pushed by NCLB and other forces toward a type of accountability that is measured by neatly bubbled exams. Yet, in a world of 21st-century demands, we need students who know how to think collaboratively, solve problems, create solutions, share widely, listen intently, and act ethically. We need students who possess literacies that are, as explained by NCTE, "multiple, dynamic, and malleable."

Indeed, we float on the edge of uncharted waters in this flat world, toward barely imagined possibilities for our students and the future they must navigate. The direction we take from here will determine that future and the destinations that await us. If our teaching is flat, our understanding insubstantial, and the experiences we offer students one-dimensional, we will fall into old ways and old results. *Bring It to Class* offers a "how-to" guide about new ways to educate that offer new results. It helps us develop the multiple, dynamic, and malleable literacies our students need. It is a guide on these uncharted waters of this flat world, one I'm glad to hold close.

—Kylene Beers, Ed.D, senior reading advisor to Secondary Schools Reading and Writing Project at Teachers College, Columbia University; president, National Council of Teachers of English; author, *When Kids Can't Read: What Teachers Can Do*

REFERENCE

Friedman, T. (2006). *The World Is Flat* (Updated and expanded ed.). New York: Farrar, Straus and Giroux.

Acknowledgments

We thank the superb colleagues who have taught us so much about researching, teaching, and learning with pop culture. These include grad students, teachers (both those studying to become teachers and practicing teachers), other teacher educators, literacy coaches, principals, media specialists, school librarians, and adolescents.

What's in Your Backpack?

Photo © Genevieve Hay

Each day my friends and I haul our own personal libraries into school. In our backpacks exists an amalgam of books: science textbooks, novels from home, novels for school. We carry phones loaded with opportunities for communication and mp3 players brimming with lyrics. Some of us even squeeze in laptops. Still, we can't carry everything. A few books lay strewn across the back seat of our cars with the occasional magazine. Sometimes, something as simple as a tattered flier, MapQuest directions, or the latest set of popular guitar chords falls between the seats to remind us of a past outing.

—Genevieve Hay, high school student, email exchange

Genevieve, who wrote her senior thesis on rock journalism as literature, is like many adolescents. The texts she uses blur across contexts. Her backpack overflows with the **21st-century** and **pop culture texts** that adolescents and adults, too, use throughout their daily lives.

Twenty-first-century texts are ubiquitous, familiar, and intuitive. They are "read," but they don't necessarily include "print." They consist of print-based material such as books, magazines, emails, and websites. But they also include visual, oral, gestural, and technological texts. They encompass informational texts, such as TV newscasts with split screens that report current events visually while other news stories stream in print across the bottom of the screen. They also include pop culture texts, which are mass-generated print and nonprint texts (e.g., comics, anime, TV shows, movies, videos, young adult books, music lyrics) that use multiple modes (e.g., linguistic, visual, aural, performative) to entice audiences to use them.

Bring It to Class is about unpacking and delving into the pop culture resources that are part of 21st-century texts in students' backpacks. Many teachers aren't quite sure how all of these texts connect to their instruction, whether it's in English language arts or math class. Take, for example, the tension Chandler Dabit feels:

It's still hard for me as a reading teacher. To me, text is still text. When it comes to testing, the bottom line is that students must be able to read written text. I know that kids are really into lots of things, and those things can be a good way to support and emphasize the written text. But I'm still a reading teacher, and I need to teach students about print.

—Chandler Dabit,
8th-grade reading teacher, interview

This book is designed to help educators reflect on long-held beliefs—that informal learning is separated, often by school walls, from formal learning; that print is the mode of choice for communicating in the classroom; and that only people with low-brow tastes engage with pop culture, while the rest of us "educated" folks distance ourselves from television, comic books, and the like, as if the plague had just announced itself.

Most importantly, this book is about connecting texts and texts that connect—pop culture texts, school texts, and texts students create—to develop the necessary competencies for 21st-century demands. Connecting texts that blur across contexts addresses

"The 21st century demands that a literate person possess a wide range of abilities and competencies—many literacies. These literacies—from reading online newspapers to participating in virtual classrooms—are multiple, dynamic, and malleable. As in the past, they are inextricably linked with particular histories, life possibilities, and social trajectories of individuals and groups." (National Council of the Teachers of English, 2008, n.p.)

the educational purposes of acknowledging and building on students' literacies in order to enable them to learn both relevant content and the thinking processes that can lead to productive and fulfilled lives.

We demonstrate how teachers use pop culture in field-tested approaches with students in grades 4–12 to connect to students' identities, to their social networks, to their belief systems, and to their **literacy learning**. Our aim is to make emerging theoretical perspectives practical for teachers.

This book is written for novice and experienced educators, classroom teachers, librarians and media specialists, coaches and administrators who want to connect to students. We include various student, educator, and researcher perspectives on pop culture in educational settings. We draw from email communications, interviews, and data transcripts to illustrate not only these different views but also how communication differs across 21st-century texts. For example, an interview transcript shows oral language while a blog posting may show conversational language and an email exchange may seem formal or informal, depending on writers' relationships to one another.

*Throughout this book, we use marginalia of different modes (images, words, charts, graphics, icons) in a textual **mashup.** Reading this book is similar to navigating the texts in our lives: where modes from text messages to snail mail to email to Internet pop-ups compete for our attention and flow from one space to another.*

Chapters include:
- *Stories of adolescents and adults engaging with pop culture*
- *Classroom instruction dubbed "Pop Culture in Action"*
- *Reflection activities for teacher study groups*
- *Annotated additional resources, including traditional and pop culture texts.*

While some educators easily incorporate pop culture texts into instruction, others find it difficult because pop culture texts often fall outside the definition of textual practices used at school. We understand that it can be hard to "wrap your mind around" a text that may have been banned in schools (like a graphic novel) or that wasn't defined as text (like a film) only a few years ago and is now promoted as central to the curriculum! Yet most educators can agree that the texts of our day-to-day lives have rapidly changed in the past 10 years, and technology has forever altered how we interact with one another and learn about ourselves and the world.

A TEXTUAL DAY IN A LIFE

Texts are important in our daily lives for reading and writing and for developing the skills to comprehend authorial intent. But it is equally crucial to understand how texts function as social practices that show identities, values, beliefs, and social networks (Knobel, 1999; Lankshear & Knobel, 2006; Street, 1995).

What do we mean when we say that texts function as "social practices"? We use texts to connect to others. For example, adolescents form friendships via pop culture. They communicate on social networking sites such as MySpace about a favorite TV show and share inside jokes that nonviewers don't understand. Texts, therefore, may be analyzed as **artifacts** that show users' identities, values, beliefs, and literacy learning in their social practices (Pahl & Rowsell, in press). Some of the texts we use at home we also use at work, for example. What are the artifacts in a student's life, in a teacher's life, or in the life of one of the authors of this book? See if you find your own textual practices connecting across the artifacts shared in the following Textual Day in a Life vignettes.

A Textual Day in a Student's Life

It is summer. Blogs, chat rooms, discussion boards, and an inflow of text messages replace textbooks. Virtual text has reclaimed its throne, for the time being. My day begins by turning on my Dell Inspiron 530 and checking (in this order) Facebook, Yahoo! Answers, and email. After perusing these online textual smorgasbords, I make my way downstairs. Here I can usually be found reading the cooking instructions for an Amy's Organic Bean Burrito. After breakfast, I watch television for hours on end—flipping channels in desperation for a noteworthy movie. Being without a driver's license, I typically must wait until 6:00, when my mother gets off work, or for an invite from a friend before I can vacate my home. These excursions consist of a visit to Grandma's, supermarket, video store, restaurant, and on occasion, social event (such as a party). When I return home, I turn on the computer, anticipating a handful of new status updates and messages. Before bed, I scan YouTube videos or download PETA podcasts, before dozing off to the soothing sounds of whatever animal is being examined at an uncomfortably close angle on Animal Planet, Discovery, or National Geographic.

—Jordan Ford, high school senior, email exchange

Table Int.1. Analysis of Jordan's Textual Day in a Life

Identities	Texts	Values	Social Networks	Literacy Learning
Student	Textbooks	Education	Teachers, students	English, math, science, history
Teenager	Blogs, chat rooms, discussion boards, text messages, email, TV	Communication	Family and friends, celebrities, others	Pop culture
Friend	Facebook	Friendship	Friends	Maintaining close bonds
Vegetarian	Amy's Organic, PETA	Healthy living, ethics, activism	Activists, vegans/vegetarians	Animal rights
Nature enthusiast	Animal Planet, Discovery, National Geographic	Conservation	Naturalists, animals	Saving the planet

A Textual Day in a Teacher's Life

I prefer to begin my day by reading the major articles in the local news-paper delivered to my door. Getting my 4-year-old ready for school in ad-dition to myself keeps me from reading the full articles. Then it's on to "My life in a hamster's wheel." On the drive to work I alternate between reading billboards and street signs, singing children's nursery rhymes to my daughter, and (I must admit) texting and emailing on my BlackBerry. Once I get to work as the head of the English/Language Arts Department, I read and respond to all pertinent departmental emails. Then, during in-structional time, I use varying strategies to improve my students' literacy levels, including comic books, Vocabtoons, SmartBoard activities, and so on. After school, I sing along to the car radio, listen to an iPod audiobook at the gym, check Facebook statuses and post comments, read and write lesson plans, and, if time permits, complete my reading of the newspaper or a novel for fun.

—Chandler Dabit, 8th-grade reading teacher, personal reflection

Table Int.2. Analysis of Chandler's Textual Day in a Life

Identities	Texts	Values	Social Networks	Literacy Learning
Citizen	Local newspaper (in print)	Current events	Community member	Headlines
Administrator	Text message, Email	Communicating	Colleagues/ ELA department	Faculty's needs
Teacher	Vocabtoons, SmartBoard, Reading and writing lesson plans	Students' literacy achievement	Education	Means of connecting students to content
Consumer	Radio songs, iPod audiobook, Reading novel	Leisure experiences Connecting with others	Others who like same songs or stories	Items of popular interest, Lives of families and friends
Parent	Facebook, Singing nursery rhymes	Language play with child	Friends and family, Parenting	Child's development of sounds, vocabulary, and story content

A Textual Day in an Author's Life

My text experiences toggle between virtual and print. At 5:00 A.M. I skim a speed tip chart inset next to the full article in *Runner's World* before heading out to meet the early-bird runners. On arriving home, I download to my iPod a podcast interview on *World Café* with Michael Franti about his new album to listen to later. I text-message our babysitter asking about her arrival time while I make breakfast. I put *March* (Brooks, 2006), a fan fiction spin-off of John March's account of his experiences in the Civil War while away from Marmee and the girls from *Little Women* (Alcott, 2004) and the pick for this month's girls' book club, by the back door as a reminder to return it to the public library. At midmorning, my computer windows open onto various worlds: Facebook status updates of long-lost childhood friends, current neighbors, and professional colleagues; a search result for scholarly articles on reading workshop implementation; an Omega Weekend sign-up for a yoga workshop in New York City; email exchanges with colleagues and my husband; and two images of my children I'm editing in Adobe Photoshop to post online. I finish the day with "family movie night," watching *Ice Age* (Wedge, 2002)—for the third time—with our sons.
    —Margaret Hagood, literacy professor, personal reflection

Table Int.3. Analysis of Margaret's Textual Day in a Life

Identities	Texts	Values	Social Networks	Literacy Learning
Athlete	*Runner's World,* Omega Weekend	Exercise/health	Runners, Yogis	Strategies for improvement
Parent	Text message, Adobe Photoshop, *Ice Age*	Scheduling, Documenting childhood, Time with children	Young adults, Children, Family	How to use texting effectively, Editing strategies, Children's humor
Teacher	Scholarly articles	Literacy education	Scholars, Students, Colleagues, Family, Friends	Methods for implementation
Woman, friend	Facebook, Podcast, *March,* *Little Women*	Connections to friends, Music, Activism, Pleasure reading	Yogis, Political activists, Music lovers, Female book club	Connections between personal and professional lives, Issues about nonviolence, Politics in Iraq, Civil War history

Reflection Activity:
What's Your Textual Day in a Life Look Like?

Use the following chart to list the texts you use throughout any given day. Think broadly about what counts as a text.

- What identities do you associate with your text choices?
- How do your text choices show your beliefs and values about literacy learning?
- What social networks are apparent from your text uses?
- How does your analysis compare to the student's, teacher's, and author's?

Table Int.4. Analysis of Your Textual Day in a Life

Identities	Texts	Values	Social Networks	Literacy Learning

WHAT'S THE HANG UP WITH POP CULTURE AND TEXTS?

While some teachers readily embrace pop culture, others are more hesitant and skeptical about how it connects to classroom learning. Can you hear yourself, your colleagues, or your students in these voices?

I wish that teachers listened to the music we like and would learn some of the dances through watching the videos. It would be really cool for a teacher to ask me how to do a dance or learn about a song. We could get to know teachers some, and teachers could get to know us some.
—Derrantae Holmes, 7th-grade student, interview

Text to me is anything that is created in any kind of symbology, whether it's words or images or a grocery list. It can be a telephone number; it can be a billboard on the highway. It can be anything from a caption to *War and Peace*. Of course text is connected to pop culture like text messaging in the digital age with all of the ways people communicate with MySpace and Vonage on the computer. The ways that we communicate now is changing the definition of text in some way. We don't have a choice. We just have to deal.
—Susan Kern, elementary, middle, and high school
ESOL teacher, interview

Using pop culture texts helps teachers to understand where the kids are coming from in this generation because there's just a gap there.
—Nadine Brown, assistant principal, middle school, interview

It depends on how teachers find out about my pop culture interests and how they use it in class. If the teacher watches and notices some things that I like, like music or sports, and then uses it in class just to get me to interact, then that is weird and stalkerish. Then the teacher is going too far. The teacher doesn't need to do all that just to get me interested in the class.
—Caroline Frangos, high school sophomore, interview

I don't look to using popular culture for its own sake. I have to see some connection to the standards, and I also have to be able to achieve some connection to it myself. Essentially, it's as much about my popular culture if not more than the students.
—Becky Haste, high school English teacher, email exchange

For many educators, pop culture presents a paradox: While its texts might bridge gaps between teachers' and students' literacy interests, schools must still be mindful of issues of appropriateness. High interest in genre and digital format can't trump content.

Bring It to Class addresses the tensions and messiness of working with pop culture, illustrating how balancing didactic lesson planning and organic inquiry can open spaces to value adolescents' texts, identities, and social networks that link learners and content. Throughout the book, we present ways to update literacy instruction in a contemporary world that is changing at a pace once thought impossible.

VIEWS OF POP CULTURE

There are three different ways to view pop culture: as **mass culture**, as **folk culture**, and as **everyday culture** (see Table 1.5).

When we engage with pop culture texts (or *any* text for that matter), we negotiate the producer's **assigned meanings** and our own **accepted meaning**, at a given point in time and place. In this way, we **construct meaning** and determine how we are going to use a text in a given context and what the text means. (See section in Chapter 1 on production-in-use for further discussion on constructing meaning.) For example, rap lyrics that seem on the surface to some users to be callous and have little socially redeeming value may hold great value for street performers who are generating revolutionary messages about social inequality. Our view(s) of pop culture influences not only how we construct meaning about a text, but how we use pop culture in our instruction.

Table Int.5. Views of Pop Culture

Mass Culture: *For the people*	*Folk Culture:* *Of the people*	*Everyday Culture:* *For and of the people*
It is assumed that audiences passively accept the text and the meanings intended by the text producer.	It is assumed that texts have no inherently produced meaning.	It is assumed that both producers and audiences hold meaning-making potential.
Pop culture texts are part of low culture, as opposed to high culture.	Pop culture is an important part of people's lives.	Pop culture is an important aspect of life, and we learn about audiences' identities and beliefs when we study text uses.
Pop culture connotes pleasure, which is unworthy of serious study.	Text study focuses on the audience's uses of texts, not on producer's intended meaning.	Study of texts focuses on the producer's intended meaning and on the audience's constructed meaning, which may differ.

Source: Adapted from Hagood, 2008

It can be challenging to change long-held views about pop culture. For example, Amy Haynie completed a 2-year professional development experience in which she learned about 21st-century texts and incorporated pop culture texts into her middle school writing classes (Hagood, Provost, Skinner, & Egelson, 2008). Yet she felt conflicted about this practice, and her views of pop culture didn't end up fitting neatly into one category.

> *Ms. Haynie views many visual pop culture texts as mass culture unworthy of study. She sees pop culture as mass culture consumption of low-brow entertainment (e.g., popular TV shows, video games, celebrity magazines, and the like) and believes there's little room for inclusion in instruction.*

Texts are only things that kids can read from rather than watch. I definitely don't think of them as visual—like movies or TV shows or other videos or other visual forms, and I don't think of texts as music either. I really have a hard time with that. Texts have to have words that can be read.

Education in my life has always been extremely important, and TV was not allowed in our home. Well, for maybe a half-hour. I am of a traditional mindset. My parents are a librarian and a high school English teacher. I was taught that we didn't learn from videos, and they were only to be used in conjunction with a book, after it had been read, like in being able to compare and contrast. So I just have a hard time with that.

—Ms. Haynie, 8th-grade writing teacher, personal reflection

Many educators feel like Ms. Haynie: Only the printed word can be deemed "text worthy." Yet when she gives writing assignments, she draws on students' unique interests and uses pop culture to help students make meaningful connections. She explained:

> *Here, Ms. Haynie views pop culture as everyday culture and connects the text to students' interests and to educational purposes.*

Their current writing assignment begins with a prompt where a girl has gone missing from a hotel room. It says, "Here are the clues. Write your story." Well, all the kids watch investigative shows on TV. Now is their chance to write about them. This is the one paper that kids turn in, and turn in on time, because it's something they're all interested in. Because they have to write it, they'll make it their own.

> *Students use investigative shows as folk culture and create their own uses for the text in the writing process. As folk culture, the audience's constructed meaning is considered authentic and is valued over the producer's meaning of a text*

She sees the value of pop culture as a resource to engage students in traditional curriculum. She uses pop culture, which she *doesn't* view as text, to help students see connections to writing, which she *does* view as text. When she links television to the curriculum, she shifts her view of pop culture from mass culture to everyday culture. This is a give-and-take view of pop culture: Texts produced by mass media do influence people's meaning making, but only to the extent that people give value to the messages the media convey. Audiences construct meaning depending on the context in which they view, read, hear, or write the text. Pop culture as everyday culture values teachers as crucial negotiators in helping students construct meaning using several different instructional models (see Chapter 2 for further discussion).

Reflection Activity:
What Are My Views of Pop Culture?

Our views of pop culture influence how we approach texts with students. As you read this book, and try out new lessons with students, we suggest you return to these questions:

- Do I see pop culture as mass, folk, and/or everyday culture?
- When does my view change?
- How does my view connect to my identities, my values, my belief systems, and my social networks?
- How does my view influence my instruction with students?
- How does my view change depending on the text discussed and the context in which I would use it?

ADDITIONAL RESOURCES

1. **Still unsure about what pop culture is?** Go to http://www.wsu.edu/~amerstu/pop/. Washington State University's American Studies program offers various definitions of pop culture in America and internationally, along with resources for exploring how pop culture gets used across cultures.
2. **What is your knowledge of pop culture?** Go to http://www.popculturemadness.com/. This website gives an overview of all things pop culture updated daily. Glance over the homepage and count how many of the news stories you already know about. Which are unknown to you? How do

those known/unknown items connect to your own pop culture interests?

3. **What are your school's and district's guidelines for using pop culture texts?** Check out your school district's website, policy manual, and curriculum guide. What do these documents say about the kinds of texts allowable in your instruction? Are there also policies specific to your school? What views of pop culture are implicit in the descriptions or specifications?

CHAPTER I

Unpacking Pop Culture

Photo of Nicole Collier © Lucy Estephanos

Skimming one of my favorite political blogs for what was likely the fifth time that day, I saw a posting with these 6th- and 7th-grade students from the Ron Clark Academy in Atlanta. They were performing a debate-style rap about the 2008 presidential candidates: "You Can Vote However You Like," a song based on rapper T.I.'s "Whatever You Like." The students confidently explained to an anchor that this wasn't a one-time activity—they regularly employed music and debate to learn. Rather than shutting popular culture out, these kids had the opportunity to embrace it and use it to refine their own voices in the name of learning.

—Nicole Collier, graduate student, personal reflection

> *Before Ms. Collier enrolled in a gradu-*
> *ate program in Learning, Design, and*
> *Technology at the University of Georgia,*
> *she was a 4th-grade (early interven-*
> *tion) teacher and a district-level model*
> *teacher leader in reading.*

As Ms. Collier discovered in this example, pop culture, when employed as everyday culture, can enliven and support a textbook's presentation of, say,
the democratic process. Pop culture texts can cap-
ture and sustain young people's attention. We have
watched them for hours at a time pore over music
lyrics, magazines, self-constructed websites, emails, video game cheat
sheets, and poems they had written (Alvermann, Hagood, Heron-
Hruby, Hughes, Williams, & Yoon, 2007). Young adult librarians,
teacher librarians, and school media specialists have reported the
same phenomenon: students' total absorption in texts that connect to
their everyday lives (Cowan, 2008; Friese, 2008). Classroom teachers,
too, have found that students engage willingly over extended periods
of time when assignments call for constructing portfolios to show-
case their multimodal stories (Vasudevan, 2006), analyzing media
messages (Hobbs, 2007), or reading graphic novels (McTaggart, 2008).

WHAT DO WE MEAN BY POP CULTURE TEXTS?

How audiences use pop culture texts—how they negotiate between **assigned** and **accepted** meanings—is described by the term **production-
in-use**. It refers to a view of pop culture as everyday culture in which
both the producer of a text and the audience have knowledge and
power over a text's meaning. When we understand the concept of
production-in-use, we stand to play a significant role in students'
learning. Imagine the learning potential in classrooms, libraries, and
media centers where students use everyday pop culture texts such as
the *Harry Potter* (Rowling, 2002) or *Twilight* (Meyer, 2005) series and
their associated movies, the latest video game, or a popular band to
say something about their own identities and perhaps even to reflect
on the identities created from their uses of these texts. Guaranteed, no
two students (or teachers, librarians, or media specialists, for that matter) will accept or take up an assigned meaning in the same way.

Differences in home backgrounds, personal interests, and past
experiences mediate the audience's meanings. Using the example of
the *Twilight* book series, some people will delight in the imaginative
language and images of the memorable characters, plots, and the like,
while others will question taboos associated with the books' attention
to witchcraft and vampires. Still others will go beyond the books to engage with multimodal texts at the official *Twilight* fan site, where books,
DVDs, and gear are readily available (www.stepheniemeyer.com).

Text no longer refers to just print-based information. Today's adolescents have grown up with "anytime, anywhere" access to texts that include, but move beyond, print. The textual landscape has changed radically in the past 20 years (Lankshear & Knobel, 2006). A quick glance at the many screens inundating us with information in grocery stores, airports, subway stations, and doctors' offices—not to mention on GPS devices, pocket PCs, cell phones, and the ubiquitous "boxes" that make up our home entertainment centers—suggests that we are living at a time in which images are pushing words off the page and screen with remarkable speed and frequency (Hull & Zacher, 2004).

But what *is* and what *isn't* a text? If young adult books, comics, movies, bands, rap lyrics, fan sites, clothing, advertisements comprised of images alone, performances (e.g., dance recitals, plays, concerts), conversations between TV news anchors, blogs, and animated cartoons are just a few examples of texts, broadly defined, is there anything left in everyday culture that isn't a text? Our answer to that question lies in the notion that audiences negotiate a producer's assigned meaning so that subsequent understanding is neither completely a producer's assigned meaning nor completely an audience's accepted meaning. If a written, spoken, or performed message is available for people to negotiate its meaning, then it *is* a text. If such negotiation is impossible (e.g., a poem written in a language such that no one in the poet's intended audience can decode the marks on the page), then it is *not* a text. However, if the poet conveyed the undecipherable text as an image, a sound, a dance, or an icon (think McDonald's golden arches) that carries meaning for the viewer or listener, then it *is* a text.

WHAT INTERESTS YOU AND YOUR STUDENTS IN POP CULTURE?

> *Questions to consider about text:*
> - *What do you like about this text?*
> - *Why do you like this text better than other texts?*
> - *Who do you share this text with?*
> - *What don't you like about the text?*
> - *Who might not like this text? Why?*

To connect meaningfully to students' pop culture passions, it's essential to first research the texts they use. The Pop Culture Survey (Table 1.1) is a collaborative project that allows teachers, librarians, media specialists, and students to study texts as artifacts. All individuals brainstorm about their interests in pop culture texts on their own, share them in small groups and as a class, and examine similarities and differences across them. This exercise can become a jumping-off point to explore texts more deeply. For instance, students can interview each other, asking questions about the text on various levels.

Table 1.1. Pop Culture Survey

Directions:

1. Consider the demographic makeup of your students in relation to their own backgrounds.
2. Complete the survey yourself (before giving it to students).
3. Request that students complete the survey, either in class or as homework.
4. You and your students share findings.
5. Guide students in analyzing similarities and differences in pop culture text preferences and uses across categories of race, class, gender, and age.

	Student demographic (Total number of students)	*Teacher, librarian, media specialist demographic*
Gender represented	____ female ____ male	
Races represented		
SES (socioeconomic status) represented		

	Teacher's interests	*Students' interests*	*Analyses of similarities and differences across race, class, gender*
TV shows			
Movies			
Music			
Best-sellers			
Magazines			
Websites			
Video games			
Trading cards			
Other (computer, shopping/ fashion, hobbies, sports)			

The Pop Culture Bag activity is another tangible means for exploring adolescents' texts as artifacts (Skinner, 2007). Teachers, librarians, or school media specialists take 5 minutes and fill a bag with some favorite texts from home. Once shared, these texts provide examples and motivation for students to fill a bag with some of their own favorites from home. This "show-and-tell" activity can focus students on making connections between identity and pop culture interests. It's also an opportunity to discuss which texts are deemed appropriate and inappropriate (and by whom) to bring to school.

> *Activities such as the Pop Culture Bag provide opportunities for teachers, librarians, school media specialists, and students to connect in a number of ways:*
> - *Intergenerational commonalities*
> - *Connections to identities and affinities*
> - *Better understanding of personal reasons for text uses*

CONNECTING POP CULTURE TEXTS TO CONCEPTS IN THE CURRICULUM

"We don't see things as they are; we see them as we are."

—Anaïs Nin

> *This quote is commonly attributed to the famous French writer Anaïs Nin (1903–1977), but it may have originated in the Talmud.*

In this chapter's opening vignette, the Ron Clark Academy (RCA) students' performance of a rap they had written struck a chord with Ms. Collier. As a former teacher and reading specialist, she recognized the motivational appeal in encouraging students to use their knowledge of pop culture (in this instance, a rap by T. I.) to express who *they* were in relation to a concept commonly taught in social studies curricula (U.S. elections). The rap format also provided students considerable practice in crafting persuasive arguments and debating, skills common in most language arts curricula.

The CNN reporter announced, "They're not old enough to vote in this election, nor even in this decade, but they're definitely mature enough to get *you* to vote." As Anaïs Nin would have predicted, these students saw possibilities for democracy from their point of view, and they expressed these possibilities in powerful ways. They debated the merits of the meanings that text producers assigned (the mass media's social and political commentaries on voting in the 2008 presidential election) and offered their alternative interpretations as youthful audience consumers. One of the RCA rappers explained in a CNN interview that the rap "doesn't necessarily show you which party to vote for, but it gives you the good and bad of both parties."

View a video of the Ron Clark Academy students' performance on CNN. Go to http://www.youtube.com and search "You Can Vote However You Like."

Pop culture texts, when viewed as part of everyday culture, convey meaningful messages that are as varied and complex as the readers, viewers, and listeners who come in contact with them. Teachers, librarians, and school media specialists who support students in their use of pop culture texts to elaborate on or to question ideas they are learning in school can create valuable opportunities for learning that might otherwise go untapped. Such opportunities need not compete with an already busy or overloaded curriculum; instead, they can complement it and make school texts more inviting, comprehensible, and memorable to students (Alvermann, 2008).

Research supports educators' interests in connecting pop culture texts to curricular concepts (Xu, 2004). For example, we know of studies that support incorporating hip-hop texts in a poetry unit (Morrell & Duncan-Andrade, 2002) and writing into video games (Burn, 2007; Squire, 2008). Think of the literacy skills involved in writing a game script, researching a backstory (the history behind a game's plot), and designing walkthroughs (directions for playing a video game).

But is there research that shows the opposite? That is, are there instances in which integrating everyday pop culture texts with the curriculum have raised a red flag that bears scrutiny? One such instance is Duff's (2004) finding that while references to pop culture during whole-group discussions enabled fully proficient English learners to make relevant connections to the school curriculum, the same did not hold for students who were learning English as a second language.

HOW DOES MULTIMODALITY FIGURE IN?

Spoken and written texts are everywhere. We often overlook how accustomed we've become to viewing them as sufficient and good in their own right. This complacency, coupled with a willingness to view linguistic texts as the primary means of teaching and learning in school, is largely out of sync with 21st-century demands of literacy learning. In everyday culture, communicating via language—that is, the spoken and written word—is, at best, partial (Jewitt & Kress, 2003).

Spoken texts are without pictures, other than those we construct as images in our mind's eye. Similarly, written texts are without sounds, except for those we imagine as we read or listen to others read aloud. In short, reading, writing, and speaking afford only a limited amount of information. Other modes of communicating (e.g., sounds, images, icons, gestures, or performances) have their own unique affordances and limitations.

A relative newcomer to the conversation on 21st-century literacy demands is the concept of **multimodality**—a way of thinking that holds text production and audience consumption accountable for the various affordances and limitations of each mode. In **multimodal texts**, different modes work together, each one complementing the other, for the purpose of adding depth and richness to otherwise one-sided texts. Multimodal texts have the advantage of distributing meaning across linguistic, visual, aural, and performative modes simultaneously, though not necessarily in that order, nor evenly across modes (Jewitt & Kress, 2003). In fact, uneven distribution is visible in the RCA students' performance. The young rappers depend largely on gesturing with their hands and bodies to convey the message that "You Can Vote However You Like." (See Figure 1.1)

Figure 1.1. Ron Clark Academy Raps "You Can Vote However You Like"

© Jenni Girtman, Atlanta Event Photography

Multimodal resources for teaching across the curriculum are available at Annenberg Media (http://www.learner.org/index.html). Look for the VoD icon to access free video.

Pop culture texts naturally connect across modes and content areas. For the younger set, consider a video documentary, such as *Charlotte's Web: How Do They Do That?* (Elbert, 2007), which demonstrates how professional trainers got the animals to "act" in the popular movie *Charlotte's Web* (White, 1952). Instruction that depends on more than one mode for communicating meaning empowers students by affording them opportunities to comprehend a range of texts based on their own experiences (Pahl & Rowsell, 2006). This is an important consideration given that 21st-century schools are sites of diverse learning opportunities—places where students often come from different geographic areas having different academic curricula and different languages.

Consider the intertextual links between RCA's rap and T.I.'s "However You Like" rap. See the children perform for T.I. at http://www.ronclarkacademy.com/news/news/ti-visits-the-academy.aspx, and then watch T.I.'s video to "vote early" at http://declareyourselfnow.blogspot.com (type in "T.I." to search the site).

Teaching with multimodal texts accomplishes more than broadening the base of students' textual experiences. It also focuses students' attention on how different texts inform or reference each other. The technical term for this kind of textual cross-referencing is **intertextuality**, a word that Julia Kristeva (1980) is credited with coining. According to Kristeva, a "text is constructed of a mosaic of quotations . . . [such that] any text is the absorption and transformation of another" (p. 66).

Of course, quotations are much more than words copied from a page or transcribed from a TV commentator's voiced opinion. Authors and TV commentators assign their own meanings when they produce written and spoken texts. For example, they carefully choose which words they'll quote, for whom, and for what purposes. Not surprisingly, such a selective process changes the meaning of a quotation even before it is offered to audiences for their interpretation. Thus, instruction that offers students opportunities to negotiate a text producer's assigned meaning in order to arrive at a personally acceptable meaning is vital to helping them become critical readers (see Chapters 3 and 4).

Reflection Activity:
Critical Reading of a Blog

Log on to Angela Thomas's **blog** (http://angelaathomas.com/) and experience firsthand how multimodal texts are key to connecting popular culture with the school curriculum. Be sure to note what is required to participate in online multimedia fiction (e.g., click on "Inanimate Alice").

> *"Inanimate Alice"* uses multimodality (images, sounds, print) to engage students in interactive online media fiction. It enables them to develop multiple literacies (literary, cinematic, artistic, etc.) while interacting in a highly participatory learning environment.

Note, as you listen to the podcast on Virtual Macbeth or engage with the **Second Life** version of *Macbeth,* the "insider knowledge" that Thomas assumes her audience will possess. Finally, jot down or discuss with a friend who has perused this website your responses to the following questions, derived from Boje (2001):

1. Who is likely to have access to Angela Thomas's blog?
2. Who has she targeted as her audience? How do you know?
3. How are parts of other texts incorporated into "Inanimate Alice"? With what effect?
4. What is selected as newsworthy for the targeted audience?
5. What are some "commonsense" or "insider" terms?
6. Which parodies, ironies, and metaphors connect to your experiences?

Pop Culture in Action:
A Blueprint for a Blogging Project

Janie Cowan is a library media specialist in Forsyth County, Georgia. She launched a blogging project for upper-grade intermediate students in her school, which served approximately 1,100 students and 112 teachers (Cowan, 2008). The idea for the project came from a 4th-grade boy's comment to her as he checked out *Frankenstein* (Grant, 2002): "You have some pretty good books in here, but why don't you have *Star Wars* [Beecroft, 2007]?" As she assured him that his request would be taken into consideration, Ms. Cowan wondered whether other students in the school might be missing their favorite texts in the school's library collection.

Thus, Ms. Cowan created a survey, similar to the Pop Culture Survey (see Table 1.1). She embedded it in a schoolwide blog. She started by learning all she could about the school district's established technology protocol. Noting that nothing is simple about gaining administrative approval when public blogging sites outside the established protocol are involved, Ms. Cowan learned how to work around the fact that she was not at liberty to use Edublog or Class Blogmeister. Consequently, she, like other educators using blogging in schools (e.g., Venters, 2009), settled on an existing district-approved blog site. It lacked the flexibility and innovative features of public blogging sites, but it served her purpose.

The day the blog went "live," the first posted question was "What is the best book you have ever read? Why?" Within 10 minutes, six teachers had responded! This told Ms. Cowan that teachers had more ready access than students to computers in the school. But it also revealed that she was likely to get teachers' endorsement of the project. As students' responses began to roll in, Ms. Cowan learned that teachers were sensitive to the issue of students' limited computer access at home; in these instances, teachers built in time during or after school for students to post.

In addition to questions about book preferences, the teachers and students blogged about book characters, preferred websites, and book authorship possibilities. During the first year of the project, Ms. Cowan noted that circulation increased substantially in the fiction books section of the library (approximately 100 books more per day). Other positive trends showed up as well, though Ms. Cowan was quick to point out that she could not formally tie these trends to blogging. Nonetheless, 2 years after the project's inception, Ms. Cowan wrote:

> The [School] Media Center Blog continues to thrive! Changes to the academic schedule have affected teachers' and kids' abilities to post during the school day, but they somehow manage to do so regardless of these obstacles. Several inquiries have come from teachers and media specialists in other school systems following the Teacher Librarian article and a presentation at Georgia's annual Library Media Conference.
> —Ms. Cowan, email exchange

This project provides evidence that working within certain school constraints did not deter either Ms. Cowan or her students from engaging with a form of pop culture that spoke to their interest in communicating about personal choices in texts. The fact that Ms. Cowan's students found ways to personalize their blog entries in spite of the blog site's restrictions on choice of font, style, and size suggests that small challenges in connecting pop culture texts to school curricula can indeed be overcome. Even significant challenges, such as those described next, seem to have workable solutions.

CHALLENGES TO USING POP CULTURE TEXTS IN SCHOOL

School policies regulate to some degree the textual activities that can go on there. For example, your school may have rules against certain kinds of text sharing and communicating. It may have filtering systems on computers that set parameters on access to popular websites (e.g., lyrics, blogs, **anime**, games, social networking). There may be lists of banned young adult novels or policies against students reading comics and graphic novels or using them to write reports. Conflicting beliefs about why pop culture texts should (or should not) be part of the school scene can spark any number of thoughtful discussions. For example, consider the following three scenarios.

To Censor or Not to Censor?

Censorship is a prevailing concern and reflects how contextually driven differences between and among interpretive communities (see also Chapter 4) can influence what counts as an appropriate text (even a single word) in one setting but an inappropriate one in another. A good example comes from Ms. Cowan's blogging project. The school-approved blog site gave her access to all of her students' posts. She had the dubious privilege of either approving or disapproving each post; moreover, she could edit any portion of a response. During the first 6 months of the project, she chose to delete two questionable posts rather than reword them. In each instance, she viewed the "offense" as having stemmed from a youthful prank or attempt to test her tolerance for language that shocks (e.g., word play that comes close to being over the top in terms of "polite" school talk).

Discussion Prompt: Do you think Ms. Cowan acted in a way that saved face for everyone? Why or why not?

Plagiarism by Any Other Name?

Remixed texts, or mashups, bring up issues of fair use. Although copying words, sounds, and images (still and moving) did not start with the Internet, online digital practices have nevertheless exacerbated the situation. Consider, for example, the fact that some forms of pop culture texts, such as **fan fictions**, depend for their effectiveness on young people's creativity in cutting, remixing, and pasting original texts. Thus, in the case of *Harry Potter and the Chamber of*

Secrets (Rowling, 2002), a fan fiction might be a new story that has Harry meeting C. S. Lewis's (1950) Peter and Edmund. Imagine a student in your school creating a fan fiction from that meeting. He or she then turns it into you for a grade.

> *Discussion Prompt:* You turn to someone else in your school to think through the situation with you. Who would it be, and why?

What Happens to Pop Culture When It's "School-ified"?

Catherine is a junior who, outside of school, reads Stephen King's horror fiction almost exclusively. Ms. Barter, her English teacher, expects students in reading–writing workshop, including Catherine, to explore other genres. In this real-case scenario captured by Chandler (2000), Catherine and her teacher are locked into a no-win struggle over who has control over reading selections in the workshop setting. As the year progresses, Catherine's expectations from her reading habits outside of school continue to clash with her teacher's expectations. Catherine makes it clear that she doesn't want to interact with other workshop participants, and she is especially impatient with plot structures other than horror fiction.

> *Discussion Prompt:* The school librarian and Catherine's teacher request a meeting with Catherine's parents. They have invited you, the principal, to join them. How will you respond?

ADDITIONAL RESOURCES

1. **Create your own mashup.** Animoto Production's website (http://animoto.com/) offers free access to several applications (including a tutorial) for creating a mashup. Once you have signed up for a free account and created your mashup, you can remix it to create yet another new text, send it as a video to friends, post or embed it online (e.g., in Facebook), or export it to YouTube.
2. **Plan a class activity that incorporates multimodal texts.** Amy Alexandra Wilson, a former middle school English/language arts teacher in Utah, likes to use a variety of texts (print-based, filmed images, sounds, and graphs) to represent the decline of the American buffalo as settlers pressed westward in the late

1800s. View a short segment from a *Buffalo Bill* DVD (available from Netflix) with your class and then discuss these points:

- What are the affordances and limitations of the multiple modes within the DVD clip? (Consider the imagery, sound, words, and body language of the text.)
- What inferences can you draw based on how the DVD portrayed Buffalo Bill, the buffalo, and you?
- Finally, read a graph depicting the decimation of buffalo herds. What are the affordances and limitations of each text? Which is more credible? Why?

3. **Respond to this finding from the Pew Internet and American Life Project.** Online literacy practices such as blogging, designing Web pages, sharing original content (e.g., artwork, photos, stories, or videos), and remixing content to create new texts are central to the lives of many young people. For example, in a phone interview study of 935 U.S. adolescents between the ages of 12 and 17 who represented a cross section of youth both socially and demographically, 64% reported participating "in one or more . . . content-creating activities on the internet" (Lenhart, Madden, Macgill, & Smith, 2007, p. i). Brainstorm a list of assignments in your content area to encourage students to apply their Internet activities to schoolwork.

CHAPTER 2

How Does Pop Culture Connect to Standards?

Photo of Chandler Dabit © Chandler Dabit

You have to make pop culture valid. If you're going to use it, you are going to take a risk. Because students are rated on their test scores, and everything can hinge on that.

—Chandler Dabit, 8th-grade reading teacher, interview

Ms. Dabit has a bachelor's degree in secondary education and English and is working on a masters of art in administration.

Ms. Dabit realizes that students bring pop culture into school every day. The challenge for educators is to determine *how* pop culture is connected to, addressed, included, and excluded in classrooms. Instruction must provide opportunities for students to think critically and to develop their facility with 21st-century texts. So, how do pop culture texts connect to standards? And why, for that matter, should teachers be interested in using pop culture to address standards?

STANDARDS INFLUENCE HOW WE VIEW POP CULTURE

Schools, classrooms, teachers, and students are bound by accountability. Across the United States, state-mandated curricular standards guide both the content to be taught and often the means for teaching it. Standards also drive content assessed by high-stakes, print-based, year-end tests that require students to read short narrative and expository passages and to answer largely factual questions. The content is often unrelated to students' lives, and the text format is one that they rarely use, unless in testing situations. This context of teaching and testing stands in contrast to the intertextual and multimodal 21st-century texts adolescents use every day. Also, instruction to prepare for these assessments habitually runs counter to the educational purposes of acknowledging and building on students' literacies so that they learn both relevant content and thinking processes in order to lead productive and fulfilled lives. Connecting standards to students' lives is paramount for their academic success.

Amanda Kochran, a middle school principal, explained:

> Making real-world connections is embedded in the standards. It's in every grade level, and that's the piece our kids don't do well on, and we talk about that across every subject. Connecting to students is where the issue lies, which is back to the whole literally comprehending text, and then being able to reuse it in a different setting. That's actually a piece that's vital to linking pop culture to achievement and standards.

However, some teachers remain reticent about pop culture and don't see its relevance for classroom instruction. As discussed in the Introduction, our views of pop culture influence how we teach with it. Those who work with adolescents need opportunities to study pop culture texts in order to move beyond an either/or divide that pits pop culture against academic learning and standards. Instead, a view of pop culture as everyday culture addresses the possibilities of text plurality, signifying that producers' assigned meaning and audiences' accepted meanings must be considered in relation to relevant social and cultural contexts.

HOW HAS POP CULTURE BEEN USED IN SCHOOLS?

In a review of a decade of research, Marsh (2008) outlined four overlapping instructional models for implementing pop culture in school. We use research from content areas in grades 4–12 to illustrate how these models play out in instruction. You may find examples of the ways that pop culture has been implemented in your own school in these depictions.

Utilitarian Model

> *Questions teachers ask when approaching pop culture from a utilitarian model include:*
> - *What pop culture texts are important to students?*
> - *How do these texts connect to schooled literacy practices?*
> - *How can I increase students' interest and content retention by connecting pop culture and standards?*

The utilitarian model focuses on using pop culture to orient students to **schooled literacy practices.** The purpose is to connect content often seen as irrelevant to students to their personal lives.

Educators like Pryor (2008) connect key content and difficult vocabulary like those in biology to pop culture examples, making the content more accessible and understandable. Melissa Venters, a middle school social studies teacher, sees clear connections to pop culture. In an interview, she said that pop culture functions "as a tool to help students comprehend better what they're reading or what they're learning, whether through the use of technology or rap music or comics."

For example, Bruce (2008) showed how four self-described struggling and low-achieving high school students used their know-how of video production of visual texts to improve their reading, writing, and textual interpretations of school-based texts. The teacher had the boys study and critique the assigned meaning of several music videos. He likened that process to composition writing and had the boys compose a music video, visually analyzing the lyrics. Students were more motivated and performed better on the task when the assignment was explained vis à vis the students' **visual literacies**.

Yet teachers must be aware of how they adopt this instructional model. Manning Pruden, a teacher featured in Chapter 5, explained in an interview: "You have to watch how you're presenting pop culture to kids, especially if using their pop culture. They might cop an attitude like, 'How dare you bring what I think is cool into a classroom or into a lesson?'" To be sure, instruction using popular culture must respect children's text uses and not trivialize their interests strictly for the sake of academic learning.

Cultural Capital Model

The cultural capital model recognizes that pop culture is closely tied to users' cultural experiences and to texts they know and love when they come to school. It values the power associated with knowledge about and ownership of particular popular texts within different groups. Instruction highlights how people use pop culture to make sense of their worlds, to gain friendships, and to connect to and exclude others. Teachers encourage students to bring texts to school that are normally ignored or omitted, such as trading cards, anime, cartoons, and comic books.

> *Questions teachers ask when approaching pop culture from this model include:*
> - *What pop culture texts are important to students I teach?*
> - *What literacies are associated with their pop culture?*
> - *How do students use pop culture to include and exclude others?*
> - *How can I connect students' pop culture to literacy learning?*

For example, Morrell and Duncan-Andrade (2002) connected high school students' urban backgrounds and interests in hip-hop music and culture to academic literacies outlined in a unit on poetry. The teachers drew on students' highly developed critical and analytical skills associated with hip-hop. They analyzed and critiqued poems and wrote poetry that incorporated the socially relevant material central to the hip-hop culture of their community. Similarly, Venters (2009) incorporated 8th-grade students' interests in blogging into a social studies unit on the Civil War. Having them blog their assignment acknowledged students' desires to network socially and to have an audience beyond their teacher. In this space, students commented about the Civil War and slavery, but they also used the blog as a forum to discuss racial issues and discrimination they had experienced.

Students often feel good about teachers' instruction that values the import of pop culture in their lives. Lauren Tourne, a 10th-grade student explained:

> I think that it's a good thing if a teacher finds out about pop culture interests and sees that it's important to us and uses it in class to make us understand [the content]. It makes me think that the teacher cares enough to really try and so the teacher really works to make sure that I learn.

Critical Model

A critical model of instruction starts from the position that pop culture texts as everyday culture should naturally be part of the

Some questions teachers asked from a critical model include:
- *What pop culture is represented in the text?*
- *Who is the intended audience?*
- *Why do audiences like this text?*
- *Who benefits from using this text?*
- *Who is left out, marginalized, or silenced in this pop culture text?*

curriculum to develop **critical awareness**. This model values connections between pop culture learning and school content (utilitarian model) and students' uses of pop culture to forge allegiances (cultural capital model). Instruction from a critical model seeks to deepen students' understandings of self and others through their analyses and probings of text, questioning how texts are produced and consumed (Alvermann, Moon, & Hagood, 1999).

Lisa Stevens (Stevens & Bean, 2007) used a critical model of instruction to deepen students' understandings about their interest in *South Park,* an animated TV show. She and Craig Weathers, the co-teacher, illustrated how students—boys in particular—enjoyed the foul language and lewd jokes in the show but also understood that some groups might be offended by this form of humor. In the students' analyses of the text, they explained how the show's writers used parody to poke fun at issues, such as political correctness.

The critical model seeks to further develop students' deep thinking about their own pop culture and how it affects them. Beth Friese, school library media specialist, noted:

> The school library supports student learning and inquiry, whether that inquiry is driven by individual interests, classroom assignments, or curiosity about the world. Including a range of popular culture in library collections, from manga and popular biographies to games, allows students to pursue their own learning in ways that are personally meaningful and relevant.
>
> —Beth Friese, email exchange

Questions teachers might ask from a recontextualized model include:
- *What texts are important to students?*
- *How do students use texts to make meaning and to connect to others?*
- *How can instruction both value students' enjoyment and transform meaning and understanding?*

Recontextualized Model

The recontextualized model incorporates aspects of the other models in a view of pop culture as everyday culture. Students learn about different perspectives of text meanings and uses to appreciate the complexity of the issues surrounding the text. However, instruction from a recontextualized model provides opportunities for students to construct new knowledge and to transform pop culture texts for new, unforeseen purposes.

Millard (2006) illustrated how a class of 6th-grade students and their teacher melded their passion for Pokémon cards and persuasive letter writing, respectively, into a transformed practice for both teacher and students. Pokémon cards had been banned from school because of recent press reports that the fad (to collect cards) corrupted youth, resulting in stealing and bullying. The teacher discussed with students their Pokémon penchant. The class then researched the various views on Pokémon discussed in the news articles. She taught students how to craft persuasive, yet balanced, letters, which they sent to the head of school, arguing for or against the school ban. Blending of school curricula with students' pop culture texts exemplifies how teachers and students create a transformative pedagogy, which Millard (2003) describes as a **literacy of fusion**.

> *Literacy of fusion is a transformative pedagogy whereby teachers make deliberate use of students' interests and meld disparate elements of school-based learning and students' pop culture such that both elements are changed. Each element makes important contributions to the other's development (Millard, 2003).*

Reflection Activity: Literacy of Fusion

"If [adults] resist the tendency to dichotomize [texts] and instead see them as a repertoire, then we can move toward understanding how engagement in any literacy practice can provide insight on an individual's literate development." (Jacobs, 2008, p. 204)

When we view pop culture as everyday culture, we use pop culture texts as part of a literacy repertoire of texts.

- Which model(s) encompass your own uses of pop culture texts?
- Which model(s) have potential to assist in teaching your content area?
- Are there any of the models you wouldn't use in the classroom? Why not?

LINKING POP CULTURE AND ACADEMIC STANDARDS

No matter what model fits your classroom best, the question remains: How does pop culture help you connect to defined academic standards for your content area? In this example lesson, Ms. Dabit drew on students' interests, validated their literacy learning, and connected pop culture with schooled literacy practices. As you read this lesson, consider the following:

- Which view(s) of pop culture does Ms. Dabit employ (see Introduction for descriptions of mass culture, folk culture, and everyday culture)?

- Which model(s) of instruction presented in this chapter does Ms. Dabit implement?
- How does pop culture connect to the stated standards in the lesson?
- How does Ms. Dabit use intertextuality and multimodality (Chapter 1) to connect content to students' lives?

Pop Culture in Action: Paul Revere Uses MapQuest

English standards addressed:
- *Comprehend print and nonprint texts*
- *Create responses through a variety of methods*
- *Use context clues to generate unfamiliar and multiple-meaning words.*

When Ms. Dabit set out to teach "Paul Revere's Ride" in the literature anthology, she knew that she had her work cut out for her. In previous years, students read the text straight through and then reread it; then she posed questions for them to answer. Yet they had difficulty meeting standards dealing with vocabulary and visualization. This year, having completed the Pop Culture Survey (see Table 1.1) with her students, she decided to incorporate students' interests in movies, graphic novels, manga, and the online tool MapQuest in her lesson.

Ms. Dabit uses standards of comprehending print and nonprint texts related to the American Revolution. She sets up students' prior knowledge to connect to vocabulary to be presented in Longfellow's poem.

Ms. Dabit began the study of "Paul Revere's Ride" by referencing excerpts of *The Patriot* (Emmerich, 2000), a movie that the students had watched in social studies class while learning about the American Revolution. She then read aloud an excerpt of *Nathan Hale: Revolutionary Spy* (Olson, 2006), a 32-page graphic novel. She made connections between Nathan Hale's life and that of Paul Revere's. She passed the book around, telling students to thumb through it and note the scenery and the characters' clothing.

Next, she read aloud "Paul Revere's Ride" as students followed along. She stopped every few lines to focus on several comprehension processes (Irwin, 2006), including summarizing, inferencing, fluency, and vocabulary building.

Ms. Dabit links the poem's vocabulary to students' understanding of instant cell phone communication, making connections between their pop culture texts and the text being read.

Ms. Dabit: One if by land, and two if by sea. [She stops reading and looks up at the class.] There is a use of code here. Remember, everyone. There is limited communication during this time. There weren't cell phones or text messaging, so they had to use something. What did he use?

Student: His lantern light.

Ms. Dabit: And his friend was waiting—where?

Student: On the opposite shore.

Ms. Dabit: [She continues reading.] For the country folk to be up and to arm. [Looks up again and walks around room.] What does that mean?

Several student at once: Weapons!

Ms. Dabit: Yes, "to arm" doesn't mean this

> *Ms. Dabit uses close reading of text to ensure students' correct vocabulary use.*

[points to her arm], but to have weapons, not body parts. [She continues reading.] Then he said "Good-night!" and with muffled oar, silently rowed to the Charlestown shore . . . [She finishes the stanza.]

Ms. Dabit: What does it mean, "to muffle"? [Silence from class.]

> *Ms. Dabit draws on students' (boys in particular) known interests in car construction.*

Ms. Dabit: [Looks around at students and waits.] What purpose does a muffler play on a car?

Student: [laughs] It quiets the engine.

Ms. Dabit: Precisely. So he's rowing a boat. When the wooden oars hit the water, it's very loud. Why is that a problem?

Student: The British will know and get him.

Ms. Dabit: Yes! [Smiles]. And why would the Brits try to kill him?

Student: Because he's going to warn the others.

Ms. Dabit: Yes, so he muffles the oars with cotton so that when they hit the water, they are quiet.

When they finished reading the poem, Ms. Dabit said, "Now, I want you all to construct your own MapQuest [map] of Paul Revere's ride. I want you to draw and label it with details, but not use lots of words. You need to include where he went and at what

> *This was a composition exercise, but students in other content-area classrooms could also create such a map using the computer. Online resources offer the opportunity for comparison of change in land use over time, for example.*

time. You can include what he felt and what he saw." As she assisted students, she prompted them to visually depict what the poem described. Calling the students' map drawings "MapQuests" cued their background knowledge of maps as something found on a computer screen, rather than unscrolled.

An example of a student's illustration (Figure 2.1) shows that not only did the students visualize the ride and recount the important vocabulary, but such a map would have helped Paul Revere, no doubt, had he been able to submit his location points and print a map in MapQuest.

Figure 2.1. Student's MapQuest Rendering of Paul Revere's Ride

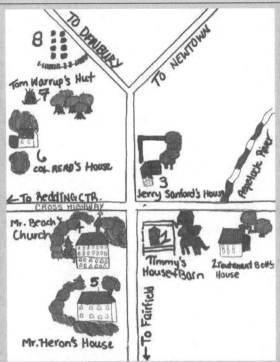

Ms. Dabit linked students' multimodal and intertextual pop culture texts to make the English curriculum relevant. Reflecting on her instruction, she noted:

Pop culture can supplement the curriculum. The more students work with text, the more they're going to understand it. So if you can do the traditional pulling out of details and main ideas, and then transfer that into a strategy where students create a new product, they'll remember even more than from just the regular classroom learning.

Reflection Activity: Understanding Visual Literacy

Imagine in your mind's eye scenes from the movie *Shrek* (Adamson & Jenson, 2001) or a comic book series such as *The X-Men*—or more traditional visual material used in schools, for example the series of photographs of the fall of Saddam Hussein's statue, likely to be found in a social studies textbook. Imagine *you* produced these texts, assigning them meaning in your choices of pictures, angles, lighting, and so on. Then answer these questions:

Search for the "Fall of Saddam Hussein's Statue" at www.famouspictures.org

> - What assigned meanings have you given to the movie or photographs?
> - What is the rationale (your beliefs, values) for your assigned meanings?
> - Who benefits from seeing this movie or photograph? Who does not benefit? Why?
> - In what other ways can you re-present what you produced?

MAKING POP CULTURE VALID

Jewitt (2008) noted that "the ways in which something is represented shape both *what* is to be learned, that is, the curriculum content, and *how* it is to be learned" (p. 241, emphasis in original). Connecting standards to students' cultural resources and investments in pop culture texts—in both print and nonprint formats—links students' lives to achievement. This good instruction, and explicit instruction in visual literacy, is effective for all students.

Ms. Dabit's quote opened this chapter, ruminating about how to "make pop culture valid." Just because pop culture is in schools isn't sufficient reason to include it in instruction. Teachers and students must define pop culture's validity through collaboration that opens up what texts are, how students use them, and how they connect to relevant curriculum.

ADDITIONAL RESOURCES

> Check out the following high school lesson plan on IRA's *ReadWriteThink* website: http://www.readwritethink.org/lessons/lesson_view.asp?id=896.

1. **Analyze the instructional models used in a pop culture lesson plan.** "You're the Top! Pop Culture Then and Now" connects high school students' contemporary pop culture to past pop culture. Read the lesson plan and discuss the different instructional models used in the lesson plan. How might you change the lesson plan to fit one particular instructional model?
2. **Experience visual literacy learning using the Library of Congress.** Go to http://myloc.gov and explore exhibits, virtual tours, online activities, knowledge quests, and lesson plans.
3. **Create personalized and customized maps that can be viewed publicly or privately at Google.** Check out the helpful video at http://maps.google.com/help/maps/mymaps/create.html.

CHAPTER 3

Connecting to Audiences, Connecting to the Canon

Photo of Jairus Joaquin © Angela Matthews

You read the history, but who's the author? —Nas

The quote from hip-hop artist Nas's song "Ghetto Prisoners" is a beckoning call for his listeners to question the information that they read and hear. . . . Although Nas creates music that discusses diverse topics such as racism, poverty, abuse, education, and history, he has also endured intense scrutiny from popular media and social critics who claim that his music glorifies violence and drug sales, promotes mistreatment of women, and contributes to the detriment of young people. Nas and other rap artists have been the subject of what is often referred to as the "hip-hop controversy."

Growing up in Detroit, Michigan, during my early adolescent years, I became engrossed in the songs of rap artists like Tupac Shakur, Nas, and Jay-Z. Tupac's voice contained so much power and passion as I listened to his words in songs that criticized the politics and capitalism of America, and spoke of the harsh realities facing poor people. Nas was an amazing storyteller who encouraged me to seek knowledge, critically assess the conditions of society, and study history. Jay-Z's linguistic capabilities astounded me. I could listen to different parts of his songs and always interpret them in a new way. He challenged me to think about the complexities of street life, to face my future without dwelling on regrets, and to create my own pathway through life.

—Jairus Joaquin, speech-language pathologist, literacy educator,
and beginning educational researcher, email exchange

Mr. Joaquin envisions the potential for hip-hop to motivate students to become critical inquirers: to challenge and question the status quo. He is committed to researching how hip-hop can galvanize young people to sharpen their **critical consciousness** about injustices in society. For Mr. Joaquin, a song's message can change depending on the part he listens to; the day, time, and place; and mood he is in. These different interpretations are his for the taking; they are signs that he is using texts in powerful ways.

> *Critical consciousness (Freire, 1973), like critical awareness, is the recognition that while economic, social, and political injustices exist in society, people are capable of taking actions against these oppressions.*

What does it take to engage students who are interested not only in what *was* but also what *is* and possibly *will be*? In our view, pop culture texts can be of help here. They connect to students' lives through inequalities and injustices that young people read from the assigned meaning of text yet believe they have little or no control over. Encouraging students to attend to such meanings, while at the same time questioning the meaning they have for their own lives, is a reasonable and responsible way to deal with pop culture in school.

As viewers, listeners, and readers who use pop culture texts differently, students will form multiple audiences for multiple texts. In Chapter 4, we'll discuss how to apply this understanding to text interpretation as typically practiced in classrooms. In this chapter, however, we focus on how students use pop culture to forge their own life pathways, much like Mr. Joaquin does, and on teachers who, being sensitive to students' interests, use these texts to complement the canon.

MEMORIZING LYRICS: IT'S ALL ABOUT COMPREHENDING

Imagine 30 young people in grades 6 through 9 in an after-school media club using pop culture in a public library. A group of girls gather around the library's two printers anxiously awaiting copies of the music lyrics they had downloaded from their favorite websites. When the copies finally spew forth (grindingly slowly), each girl grabs her copy, rushes to the nearby vacant auditorium, and joins her friends in practicing for performances that often required lengthy and repeated rehearsals until the lyrics were memorized perfectly (Alvermann et al., 2007).

> *"Lyrical poetry is out for the time being, and something that is called rap or hip-hop is in. It is still poetry, and we can't live without it. We need language to tell us who we are, how we feel, what we're capable of—to explain the pains and glory of our existence."—Maya Angelou*

The girls' monopolizing of the Internet and printer was an aggravation for the library staff. However, other adults in their lives saw educational value in the girls' desire to read and memorize the lyrics of popular artists. One girl's mother, for instance, noted in an interview that reading lyrics had a definite advantage over merely listening to them:

> You could listen to a song a hundred times and you listen to it and you say, well, I know what it saying. But if you read it you know what it saying. I mean, 'cause you read it, you like, oh, I didn't know it say *this* part. If you read it, you comprehend it.

She, too, had memorized poetry as a young girl for many of the same reasons, adding that, in her opinion, young people acquire academic concepts more readily when learning is made fun.

We agree. A generation of children in the 1970s and 1980s (Margaret and Alison included) remember much about multiplication facts, grammar rules, functions of the body, and the workings of government through *Schoolhouse Rock*. This series of 41 animated shorts aired between Saturday morning cartoons for 12 years on ABC TV. Wikipedia provides a history of the series, which originated when a man in an ad agency noted that his son knew every lyric the Beatles and Rolling Stones had ever written yet couldn't master something as basic as the multiplication tables. His solu-

> *Search for Schoolhouse Rock on YouTube (www.youtube.com) to view 3-minute videos of the catchy tunes and goofy characters that teach basic facts about a variety of subjects.*

tion? Link math content with contemporary music and engaging graphics. The idea expanded to include other subject areas, thus securing *Schoolhouse Rock* (Warburton, 2002) a place in schools, even to this day.

Memorization is a respected though often disputed practice in education circles. The same can be said for pop culture texts, especially when viewed as edutainment (a contracted form of *education* and *entertainment*). Critics of edutainment claim it has little to offer young audiences beyond teaching them that they can acquire information with minimal effort and study on their part. For more than a decade, these critics (e.g., Carlson & Apple, 1998; Okan, 2007) have viewed pop culture as mass culture and questioned the wisdom of aiding and abetting young people's interests in texts that put serious learning at risk. Less pessimistic views of edutainment suggest that young people's learning potential is not slowed by their engagement with pop culture texts (Short & Kaufman, 2000). In fact, we know of three high school chemistry teachers who used *CSI*-related materials (Donahue & Zuiker, 2000) to teach about scientific inquiry (Guzzetti, 2009). Rather than discouraging serious study, *CSI* resources (e.g., selected TV episodes on video, mystery game scripts, detective novels, and books on forensics that they downloaded to their iPods) actually motivated students to deepen their study of forensic science.

GOING BACKSTAGE WITH STUDENTS

Matthew (Matt) Bryant is a middle school English/language arts teacher who enrolled in Donna's online content literacy course. Teachers used the online class discussion board to learn from one another. In response to an assigned reading of Weinstein's (2007) article "A Love for the Thing: The Pleasures of Rap as a Literate Practice," teachers noted that pop culture texts are not difficult to find in their schools; they are everywhere. But finding the time and support needed to plan instruction around such texts was challenging. Mr. Bryant explained it this way:

> Many times, educators ask themselves, how will I ever get through to this kid? My answer is that I feel that in order to teach you must go backstage and find out students' feelings and interests, being mindful that learning should be connected to their social experiences. We live in a media-driven world where entertainers have a significant influence on the cultural identities, norms, and beliefs of many adolescents. Music has historically been a source of significant influence on youth of different cultures, classes, and gender.
>   FYI: There are different types of rap.

> *Mark Lamont Hill's (2009) book* Beats, Rhymes, and Classroom Life: Hip-Hop Pedagogy and the Politics of Identity *expands on the ideas presented here.*

1. Gangsta rap
2. Materialistic rap
3. Political/protest rap
4. Positive rap
5. Spiritual rap

All types have their pros and cons. Overall, if utilizing a child's interest in rap music to communicate important lessons in life is what works in your classroom, why not go for it. I believe that if educators use or at least understand rap music, [it] opens a door of communication that allows students to have authentic conversations.

—Matt Bryant, middle school teacher, course discussion board post

Pop Culture in Action:
Connecting Rap Lyrics to a Unit on Bullying

Lark Zunich, a middle school reading teacher in California, captures some of the instructional routines he uses when teaching a unit on bullying that incorporates the popular young adult novel *Holes* (Sachar, 1998). The following is adapted from Mr. Zunich's chapter in *Trading Cards to Comic Strips: Popular Culture Texts and Literacy Learning in Grades K–8* (Xu, 2005). Mr. Zunich uses a combination of direct instruction and an adapted version of literature circles to frame his daily lessons. He begins each class with a check of the student planner, which consists of student-written objectives and ideas for homework assignments. He also requires that students complete a comprehension activity daily and log a minimum of 100 hours of reading per week.

Next comes a 5-minute warm-up activity that provides fluency practice in shared readings from a small segment of a class text, such as *Holes* (Sacher, 1998), to develop appropriate intonation, phrasing, and pronunciation. After the warm-up, Mr. Zunich uses comprehension strategies that activate students' prior knowledge about a topic (e.g., bullying, one of the injustices that Stanley, the main character in *Holes*, experienced) and provides practice in making predictions, drawing inferences, visualizing, and summarizing.

In a lesson designed to challenge his students to read raps for their social messages, Mr. Zunich had them tell the themes their favorite music artists usually rapped about. When some students couldn't identify a theme, he suggested they think about the rapper's *big picture* or *major message*. They could also confer with a partner about the theme or message. Then they copied or printed lyrics from their favorite websites and entered information from those lyrics into a four-box journal constructed by folding a sheet of paper into quadrants. In box 1 they wrote a summary of the lyrics; in box 2 they recorded interesting words from the lyrics; in box 3 they posed discussion questions; and in box 4 they made intertextual connections (e.g., to *Holes*).

The four-box journal provided a place for students to demonstrate that they had comprehended the text, and it could be used later in literature circle. The four-box journal could also be used to record information from a chapter in *Holes* that might then be compared and contrasted with rap lyrics that also reflected themes of bullying, injustice, and oppression. We like Mr. Zunich's four-box journals for both rap lyrics and popular novels because it provides opportunities to analyze how the same rap or book can evoke different responses, depending on who the readers are, their previous experiences, and their sense of what is fair or unfair in life. Anticipating different responses from different audiences—whether on social justice themes or in relation to the canon—is vital to planning lessons around pop culture texts.

Pros and Cons of Using Rap in the Classroom

Table 3.1 summarizes some of Mr. Bryant's classmates' responses to his post. Their postings show that teachers are an audience for rap music, just like their students. They also offer a range of views on the pros and cons of rap music. Over half of all responders mentioned that they drew on personal experiences with rap music or, in the case of the literacy coach, on the talks she had with her son about his interest in rapping.

Using Pop Culture Novels to Complement the Canon

Emily Pendergrass, a part-time English/language arts and reading teacher in rural Georgia, found her middle school students' interest in reading the canon-sanctioned novels at her grade level wane considerably with each passing year. She wrote an article on the subject (Pendergrass, 2008), noting that her students spent hours poring over magazines, instant messaging, and using skills learned in school to blog and impress their friends on Facebook but counted the minutes during her English/language arts class until the clock signaled the end of another school day.

Table 3.1. Teachers' Pro and Con Statements About Rap Music

Subject-Matter Teachers and Specialists (Grades 4–12)	*Pro*	*Con*
English/language arts	Appreciation for the ebb and flow of the hypnotic rhythms that are unique to rapping	Violence, sexuality, blatant lack of respect for authority
Science	Lyrics showing people's struggles aren't that far removed from those displayed in textbooks	Degrading lyrics that result in students having to check their lives/world at the classroom door
Mathematics	A pathway for teachers to show that they value kids' interests, expertise, and choices	A potential for isolating oneself in a smaller community as opposed to communicating on a more global level
Social studies	A way of balancing kids' interests with more traditional skills needed to meet standards	Unfamiliarity with rap and hip-hop lifestyle among some teachers (meaning inability to assist students)
Speech therapist	Encourages people to voice their opinions, tell a story, and relay information using figurative language	Getting lost in the music and not really listening to the words/lyrics of the song
Literacy coach	A means of establishing some common ground with students and staying on top of what interests them outside of school	Doesn't like the violent rap, but if students choose to listen to it, so be it; just have to hope they know how to separate it from the reality of their lives

Rather than ignore a worsening situation, Ms. Pendergrass built a classroom library of books that appealed to students' interests in pop culture while not totally discounting what she valued as a teacher. She introduced students to books that rewarded thinking critically about various elements, characterizations, and plot developments regardless of the genre. But with only so much time in the school day, Ms. Pendergrass, like many teachers, felt the need to justify spending instructional time on pop culture texts.

This need to juggle students' interests with a standardized curriculum is real and often made more complex by the fact young people are frequently fans of pop culture texts thought to be entertaining but lacking in any real substance. The importance of defending students' choices to building and district-level administrators, to say nothing of parents, was something that Ms. Pendergrass took seriously. She devised a plan that enabled her to show the qualities of pop culture texts that related to the canon and yet genuinely tapped students' interests. Table 3.2 lists those qualities for three young adult novels that were popular among her students. Note the extension activities that Ms. Pendergrass lists. How might you adapt these for use with students in your school?

CENTER STAGE: ADOLESCENTS AUTHORING TEXTS FOR PEER AUDIENCES

Generally, literacy experts tend to view reading and writing as two sides of the same coin but heavily weighted in favor of reading—a

Table 3.2. Pop Culture Novels for an Audience of 21st-Century Adolescents

Title	Why It's a Pop Culture Text	Description	Extension Activities
L8r, g8r Lauren Myracle (2007)	Computer screens for pages; different fonts for different characters. Spelling and syntax use IM and text messaging conventions. Emoticons, *actions* indicated by asterisk enclosures.	Last in a trilogy of novels written in the form of IM and text messages. Storyline focuses on boys, gossip, and revenge.	*L8r, g8r* lends itself to the creation of song playlists mentioned in the novel. Note the shifts in voices and perspectives of the three main characters based on the texting conventions the author uses.
Blue Bloods Melissa De La Cruz (2006)	Multigenre twist with a full-length narrative plus fictional journal of a 1620s vampire who is still alive. Delights an audience that likes dropping brand names and reading about celebrities.	Plays off popularity of vampire lore. Plot involves youth whose lineage dates back to Plymouth and their attempts at finding out who or what drained the blood of their vampire friends.	Rewrite *Blue Bloods* from the perspective of another vampire. Compare and contrast social-class differences and myths surrounding vampires.
The Game of Sunken Places M. T. Anderson (2004)	Authentic gaming situations populate this book. Includes excerpts of a game dialogue between the two main characters.	Two boys stumble on an old game that becomes their lived reality. Their goal is to win the game before time is up or before they succumb to a series of encounters with ogres, ghosts, and trolls.	Discuss whether or not it is appropriate and useful to apply game ratings to *The Game of Sunken Places*. Critically examine other games in relation to *The Game of Sunken Places*, looking for elements of authenticity in language, setting, and costumes.

> Lynell Burmark—teacher, administrator, and advocate of visual literacy—writes: "It's time not only for students to read or consume images, but also to write or produce them in ways that let [their] values, feelings, and achievements take center stage." (Burmark, 2007, p. 23)

notion that Andrew Burn (2007) thinks is worth a second look. He studies young people's production of popular media texts for an audience of their peers. Young media producers spend considerable time authoring popular texts. They learn how to refine their compositions to address different audiences, whether they are writing for comic strip fans, graphic novel readers, or gamers. They are also adept at refining other authors' texts. For example, the students at Ron Clark Academy (Chapter 1) adapted rapper T.I.'s "Whatever You Like" to make it acceptable to audiences of voting age. These sophisticated moves on the part of learners who have access to free or relatively inexpensive software indicate that young people are more than mere consumers of pop culture texts; they are producers as well. This is evident in the case of student-authored fan fictions and video games.

Fan Fiction

As noted briefly in Chapter 1, fan fictions (such as *Twilight* [Meyer, 2005] or *Buffy the Vampire Slayer* [Whedon, 1997–2003]) are stories that admirers of an original work write by using the

> To gain a sense of the audiences and communities that develop around young people's engagement with fan fiction, from fans of anime/manga, books, cartoons, comics, games, movies, plays, and TV shows, visit http://www.fanfiction.net/.

settings, characters, and plot from the original to create different situations and endings. Drafts undergo reviews by peers, who are often quite explicit about their criteria for evaluating the impact of a particular piece. Finished pieces circulate within online peer affinity spaces where novices and experts interact, often exchanging roles, depending on the activity or context at any given time (Black, 2008).

> For ideas specific to the literacy and composition practices of English learners in an online fan fiction community, read Rebecca Black's 2005 article in the Journal of Adolescent & Adult Literacy.

Student authors of fan fiction have audiences in mind when they create stories that challenge dominant representations of gender, ethnicity, and sexuality in the media (much like the focus of the critical model of instruction described in Chapter 2). This critical component can focus whole-group discussions during a lesson on critical media literacy. See Figure 3.1 for suggested activities for focusing and following up on the discussion.

Figure 3.1. Authoring with an Audience in Mind: Fan Fiction-esque Activities for Critical Media Literacy Discussions

---

Things that teachers, school librarians, or media specialists might look for in critical media literacy discussions include the following:

- Why fan fiction authors may choose to recontextualize an original storyline
- Why they may cast one of the female characters as an action-adventure heroine
- Why they may cast a person of color as the main protagonist

If you have fan fiction authors in your room, ask if they would be willing to share one of their pieces with the class. Alternatively, you can select an appropriate story from www.fanfiction.net. A popular category is TV shows. Find out students' favorite shows and then choose a story that will support discussion of the above items.

As a follow-up activity, have students create prequels, sequels, and/or alternative endings for media texts they choose.

Discuss why these sorts of activities can encourage students to be more critical consumers of mainstream media messages. They may also expand students' thinking about how mass media shapes the possible roles available to them.

Source: Adapted with permission from Black, 2008.

Video Games

It may be hard to swallow, but video games do have a place in school and literacy learning (Gee, 2003). In fact, **game literacy** is more than a fashionable metaphor. It includes writing scripts, researching and authoring backstories (the histories behind various game plots), and producing walkthroughs (video-captured directions for winning the games) (Burn, 2007). Students who are producing their own games and authoring them as texts are (in the process of) learning sought-after media job skills for a 21st-century literacy demands.

> *Interested in adding games to your instructional repertoire? Check out* Cable in the Classroom *magazine (www.ciconline.org/cicmagazine). Type "Windward" in the search box and discover a free video game that lets students outsmart the weather in a race around the world.*

TEXTS THAT CONNECT: OR DO THEY?

Defining what is worthwhile or practical about using pop culture texts in literacy instruction will vary according to our views of pop culture and our experiences of connecting academic texts to students' everyday lives. This is important to keep in mind as you read the two vignettes in preparation for the reflection activity that follows.

Vignette #1: Whose Vocabulary Counts for Which Audience?

Tracey Kell, a library media specialist for a school in Georgia with a large number of English language learners (ELLs), responded to a classmate's posting on a discussion board in one of Donna's online courses. The classmate had pointed to the difficulties ELLs experience when their knowledge of pop culture interferes with their comprehension of academic texts. Ms. Kell wrote back:

> Your ELL students reminded me of a story from last year that illustrates cultural and linguistic bias [in testing]. A 7th-grade ELL language arts teacher was very upset regarding a reading passage on the benchmark (formative) test. It was about a "policeman on a beat with his club." Her students all associated the word *club* with a nightclub and *beat* with music. They had no clue what the passage was about!

Vignette #2: How Do I Say What I Need to Say?

Carla Hunter, a middle grades math teacher in Georgia, posted this response to a class discussion board after reading Vasudevan's (2007) article on multimodal literacy practices:

> I have found that most of my students are more than happy to converse about any subject, but the moment I ask them to put their thoughts on paper they develop writer's block. Since their "speaking text" flows much more freely than their "writing text," it may be a helpful tactic to allow them to record their free-flowing thoughts on a tape recorder and then transcribe these thoughts into text.

For Ms. Hunter's students, writing by itself did not offer the support they needed to communicate their thoughts. Other communicative modes—spoken language and listening to what they recorded on tape—were necessary for **scaffolding** the writing process.

Reflection Activity: Fractured Expectations and Experiences of Text

These teachers' vignettes demonstrate a "fracturing" of what the audience (a group of middle school students) understood about the texts they were assigned to read or write. The fracturing "disconnected" the students from what schools, tests, and teachers expected them to learn or create in these contexts. In the first vignette, pop culture texts that connected to students' lives became a source of confusion when they failed to recognize in a testing context that a policeman's club was not a nightclub, nor was his beat related to music. In the second vignette, the "fracture" occurred at the juncture between the students' expectation that oral communication was sufficient and the teacher's expectation that written communication was the desired end product.

1. How would you have handled the situation if you were the teacher in Ms. Kell's vignette?
2. If you had been Ms. Hunter, how might you have assisted the students?
3 Do either or both of these vignettes cause you to question the advisability of using pop culture texts in academic settings? Why or why not?

ADDITIONAL RESOURCES

1. Search for Dana Kling's Grammalyrics #1 on YouTube to see how a high school English teacher uses pop culture to motivate his students to use proper grammar. Does Mr. Kling know his audience? What evidence in the video supports your opinion?
2. Reread Table 3.2, Ms. Pendergrass's plan for starting a classroom library of pop culture novels. What book would you recommend she add? Provide a rationale for why it fits the genre of pop culture novels, and suggest at least one extension activity.
3. Find a video game that appeals to you and then evaluate it for the following:
   * Evidence of a well-researched backstory
   * Accuracy of the walkthrough
   * Authenticity of props, clothing, and language use
   * Potential for connecting to a school's curriculum

CHAPTER 4

Connecting Pop Culture to Text Interpretation

Photo of Travis Cooper © Cindy Cooper

I currently teach world history during the Middle Ages in an urban high school in Washington, D.C. Most of my students read below their grade level, live below the poverty line, and have difficult home lives and think of social studies, and the skills it teaches, as irrelevant.

One of my objectives is to have students piece together facts about an event after viewing multiple sources. For one lesson, I brought in a variety of documents about the scandal between Chris Brown and Rihanna, two well-known hip-hop artists. Some of the documents included a police report from the alleged assault by Chris Brown on Rihanna, a gossip article from TMZ.com that claimed to have all the facts, a police photograph of Rihanna after the assault, and public statements from both artists after the incident. I broke students into groups and had them list all the

> *Here Mr. Cooper is referring to an alleged domestic violence incident that received widespread media attention.*

facts they could find after reviewing the sources. The results were amazing. Every group had a different list of facts with some commonality. Many groups showed bias toward one of the artists, and some groups favored sources such as TMZ.com or the artist's public statements over the police report and photograph. We used this dissonance to begin a conversation about how historians collect information about an event and how they distinguish between what is fact and rumor.

—Travis Cooper, high school social studies teacher, email exchange

Travis Cooper uses pop culture to help students realize that interpreting events requires reviewing multiple accounts—critically. In this chapter we show how pop culture can help educators engage students in challenging interpretation practices—such as critical analysis of sources—that are part of school learning. Similar to the idea of intertextuality and multiple interpretations that we discussed in Chapters 1 and 3, the teachers in this chapter intertwine several different texts to help build students' content knowledge, to invite diverse perspectives, and to incorporate students' own uses of text into the curriculum.

Consider this second example, in which Greg Roach, a high school social studies teacher, used song lyrics to move students beyond viewing the practice of history as the detached study of facts. Mr.

> See *http://en.wikipedia.org/wiki/Kenji_ (song)* for more information and *http:// www.metrolyrics.com* and search for "Kenji" to view the lyrics.

Roach played the song "Kenji" (Fort Minor, 2005) to help his students empathize with Japanese Americans who were placed in internment camps during World War II. Family members of the lead signer, Mike Shinoda, were imprisoned in camp Manzanar. The musical intertextual collage integrates clips from a real interview with his father and aunt and lyrics telling a fictional story of a man named Kenji, an immigrant who experienced discrimination after he was released from the camp.

The genre of this musical text invited varied interpretations because of its multifaceted structure. By using a pop culture text, Mr. Roach guided students to interpret historical events through an aesthetic experience—readings that emphasize emotion and personal perspective—rather than through the presumably factual (and most likely dry and standoffish) third-person prose of a social studies textbook, lecture outline, or typical study of a young adult novel about the subject.

WHAT IS INTERPRETATION?

Interpretation is a content-specific endeavor that looks differently across teachers and subjects. When, for example, an English teacher asks his 7th-grade class to interpret the Langston Hughes (1995) poem "Dream Deferred," students can expect a familiar range of options. Perhaps they must answer a list of questions on imagery and metaphor from the class literature anthology or write a journal response relating their own life experience to a theme depicted in the poem. In an 11th-grade American history class, the teacher might ask students to analyze primary source documents from the Revolutionary War and to discuss which one carries the most credibility based on its corroboration with other documents. Interpretation involves a set of practices defined by context that gives a person information as to how to go about treating a text.

We define *interpretation* as the act of searching for understanding, a reconciling of what seems obvious and transparent to a reader at a given point in time and what the reader perceives to be still unknown. Thus, **interpretation** is necessarily problem-based and involves such behaviors as deciphering, clarifying, articulating, and unraveling across and within texts. Because interpretation is an ongoing process, multiple and changing perspectives across time and people are possible. We take our definition from the work of Richard Shusterman (2000), who has examined how people interpret cultural texts as artifacts, such as hip-hop and country music. He wrote, "We seek an interpretation because we are not satisfied with the understanding we already have—feeling it partial, obscure, shallow, fragmented, or simply dull—and we want to make it fuller and more adequate" (p. 132).

Interpretive Communities

One challenge in guiding students through an interpretation is deciding where you want them to end up. Doing so will help you decide how pop culture texts fit into your curriculum. For example, do you want students to come to an already-established conclusion, one that is widely accepted in a particular content area, such as life sciences? Or do you want students to explore several different possibilities? Because interpretation is a content-specific endeavor, your answer to these questions might depend on the subjects with which you have had the most experience and success.

However, it might also depend on your teaching style—whether, say, you prefer **inquiry** or direct instruction. Finally, your answers are influenced, too, by your views of pop culture (see Introduction) and by the instructional model(s) (see Chapter 2) that best match the standards within any given lesson plan.

> *"My vision for how interpretation would be beneficial in science class and consistent with the scientific inquiry in which scientists engage would involve having students interpret self-generated data to validate their support or refutation of a theory or idea."*—Todd Campbell, *assistant professor of science education, Utah State University, email exchange*

For Stanley Fish (1980) an **interpretive community** is a group of people tightly connected around a set of interpretive principles, or rules, that govern how interpretation is performed and how meaning is assigned. Interpretive communities, then, involve the variable ways in which people can use and understand texts, and thus work well when trying to grasp how students use all texts, including pop culture texts, because the rules are always context-dependent. In a high school English class, for example, the rules are often determined by **New Criticism**, which requires a close reading of a text and attention to literary devices such as irony and allusion. In a media center, the media specialist may work within guidelines for assessing the credibility of an online source document or finding books for pleasure reading. These community guidelines differ, so the ways in which members approach texts will also differ.

How might interpreting a text while reading for pleasure look different from interpreting a text used in class while following a teacher's directions? Interpretive communities can certainly overlap. For example, when students read a novel for English class, they may well read to answer a set of teacher-designed questions or to study for a quiz. At the same time, they may enjoy the novel, relating it to their own experiences and turning the pages to find out what happens next. The same might happen in social studies, where students could read Internet texts to answer their own inquiry questions about the Vietnam conflict while also looking for names and dates for a time line they will construct with their classmates regarding the events leading up to America's involvement. At least two different kinds for reading, then, take place, for two different interpretive purposes. In the first case, reading in social studies is about satisfying a personal curiosity. In the second case, it is about gathering discrete bits of information for later collaboration and, ultimately, a conceptual understanding of an event in history.

Diversity of Interpretations

One assumption about interpretation commonly held is that a text holds key assigned meanings and the reader must uncover the author's intent, using the text as the primary reference. You might hear an English teacher say to students something like, "I will accept any interpretation so long as it is supported by evidence from the text." Faust (2000) uses a courtroom metaphor to explain how this functions: The teacher and students study the text for the facts of the case—the evidence—and cross-examine the text to unlock hidden assigned meanings.

Another approach to interpretation—what could be referred to as a multicultural or multiple-perspectives approach—builds on readers' cultural and social experiences. Like the critical, cultural, and recontextualized models of instruction described in Chapter 2, this approach to interpretation treats pop culture as everyday culture. Texts are not stable reference points with a set of predetermined meanings that can be uncovered, or unlocked, if only the words on the page are paid close enough attention. Instead, interpretation allows for a number of different spins on a text. The interpretive community and the identities members have of themselves within the community determine constructed meaning and text uses.

Pop Culture in Action: "The Freshman"

Find the lyrics to "The Freshman" at http://www.thelyricsarchive.com/lyrics/thefreshman.shtml

Take, for example, a lesson plan on the song "The Freshman" by the Verve Pipe that was co-developed by Vicky Wuerfel, a pre-service teacher in one of Alison's English methods courses; Ms. Wuerfel's daughter (age 13) son (age 11); and two of their friends (ages 13 and 15).

In the lesson, the interpretive community takes seriously the readers' constructed meanings that change with the various social and cultural experiences they bring to the text.

Lesson Objectives:

1. Students will analyze the text in small groups using interpretive communities.
2. Students will collaborate as a class and evaluate the text to try to locate a meaningful story within the song lyrics [written by the Verve Pipe band member Brian Vander Ark (1996)].
3. Students will defend, dispute, disprove, and reevaluate their

assumptions about the text based on input from other interpretive communities as well as the author of the text.

During the lesson, the teacher first engages the students in a discussion of the interpretive communities that make up their points of view as readers. She asks them to record those communities on a worksheet. The teacher lists his or her own communities as well. Ms. Wuerfel, for example, listed "technical writer, volleyball player and coach, mom, and future English teacher." Her daughter, Alaina, listed "14-year old, musician, and volleyball player." After reading the lyrics silently, the students and teacher add any communities that they believe they left out on the original list but that they then realize affect how they interpret the lyrics. Alaina, for example, listed "watches medical shows" (one interpretation of the song lyrics is that they depict an abortion).

Next, the class members discuss what they think the lyrics mean and add any additional communities to their list that they deem relevant after hearing one another's comments. More are added after watching the music video of the song, and final ones are added after reading the composer's lyric citations.

> See Brian Vander Ark's lyric citations at http://songfacts.com/detail.php?id=2474

Finally, the teacher and students discuss how they changed their minds about relevant interpretive communities as they traveled through the multiple representations of the lyrics (independent reading, class discussion, video, and composer's citations). Ms. Wuerfel, for example, added "Catholicism" to her list after she read the composer's notes and realized that he meant the song to be about an abortion. The lesson, then, is not about finding an interpretation based on the facts of the text but rather about examining how a text changes in significance depending upon the interpretive community and how the text is represented (e.g., visually or linguistically).

Reflection Activity:
Interpretive Communities in the Content Areas

1. What teaching styles most appeal to you? Inquiry? Collaborative learning? Lecture? Discussion? Think about how these styles affect how you expect students to interpret texts in your class.

2. What theories (such as social constructivism, feminism, or New Criticism) frame instruction in your content area or specialty and affect your expectations for interpretation?
3. What are some of the guidelines for an interpretive community that go hand-in-hand with these theories? How might pop culture texts fit in with these guidelines?

POP CULTURE AND CONCEPTUAL UNDERSTANDING

Students have a deeper conceptual understanding of content-area subjects as a result of interpreting texts. The educational psychologist Rand Spiro and his colleagues have argued that a student's ability to apply instructed knowledge to novel situations denotes complex conceptual understanding of material (Spiro, Coulson, Feltovich, & Anderson, 1988). Spiro and Jehng (1990) refer to the instruction that leads to such application, or knowledge transfer, as **random access instruction**. This instruction involves providing students with multiple multimodal representations of a concept—in the form of explanations, analogies, and other dimensions of critical thinking—so that the students revisit the concept from a variety of vantage points. Pop culture texts can be used to this end.

For example, Jessica McCarthy, a high school English teacher in northern Virginia, uses pop culture to teach literary criticism. Ms. McCarthy described the process this way:

> When teaching literary criticism for the first time, the students have a hard time understanding how to apply the techniques to literature. After reviewing the various literary criticism lenses, I show them music videos and analyze them using the applicable literary criticism points of view. (For example, I show Pink Floyd's "Another Brick in the Wall: Part I" [1979] to show symbolic, psychological, moral, and historical/biographical criticism. I use Faith Hill's "The Way You Love Me" [2000] to show feminist and archetypal criticism.) In preparation for their application to a text, each student chooses a music video of their choice, and presents it to the class while investigating it using literary criticism. The students enjoy watching the videos and they can easily relate to them, making the focused analysis easier. By having the students present to the class, the rest of the students are able to see the skill modeled again and again. Students then revisit the critical perspectives during the year using more traditional literature texts, such as Macbeth and The Taming of the Shrew.
>
> —Jessica McCarthy, email exchange

Pop Culture in Action: The Day the Earth Stood Still

How does random access instruction look in other content areas? This 6th-grade science lesson think sheet designed by teacher Bill Sidenstick is taken from an earth/space relationship unit. Students must distinguish the features of different planets in our solar system as one objective of the unit plan. Consider the following as you read the think sheet: What are the content-specific interpretive practices this lesson asks of students? How might using this think sheet (see Figure 4.1), along with the pop culture film *The Day the Earth Stood Still* (Wise, 1951), help you foster random access instruction about planets differently (or more effectively) than if you presented the lesson as a lecture?

> One possibility is that this think sheet fosters the interpretive practice of noting the features of living creatures and their environments as one reads (or views) text.

Figure 4.1. Think Sheet Prompting Students to Consider What Life Is Like on Another Planet

Name _____ Date _____ Period _____

The Day the Earth Stood Still

The Day the Earth Stood Still is a famous science fiction movie—the most famous of its day (1951). As you watch the movie, listen for information that will help you answer the following questions:

1. What was the alien's name? _____

2. What was the robot's name? _____

3. What type of spacecraft did the alien use to come to Earth?

    _____

4. In what city did the spacecraft land? _____

5. Describe the alien's physical features or appearance:

    _____

    _____

6. What does the alien say about what his planet is like or how far away it is?

    _____

    _____

POP CULTURE AS INTERPRETATION

Texts can be integrated into any content-area classroom when teachers treat pop culture as a set of intertextual and multimodal texts that connect across contexts. Pop culture, though, is more than a set of texts—it is also a set of social practices (as discussed in the Introduction) that governs how those texts get used. Adolescents use song lyrics, digital social networking, YouTube, and the like in very different ways than the teachers featured in this chapter outline, as evidenced by the stories of adolescents' connections to pop culture offered throughout this book, such as Timony's affinity for Kurt Cobain (described in Chapter 5). What sort of literacy learning should guide interpretation, then, when pop culture become the focus of interpretation in a classroom rather than a supplement to (or catalyst for) routine content-area learning? If an English teacher wants to use a popular film as a subject for literary analysis, or if a social studies teacher wants students to discuss how current images in the popular media represent particular ethnic groups, one possibility is that the students will resist the application because it interferes with the pleasure they take in the text. As with the instructional models described in Chapter 2, we must acknowledge students' pop culture pleasures. However, pop culture as everyday culture includes interpretive practices of both mass culture and folk culture. Interpretive practices that move students beyond pleasure and experience must put them in a state of cognitive dissonance. Mr. Cooper illustrated this practice in this chapter's opening vignette when he had students interpret the altercation between Chris Brown and Rihanna, two famous celebrities students liked. Simply acknowledging or allowing students' pleasure is not enough (Alvermann, Moon, & Hagood, 1999).

This resistance can be a good thing for classroom learning, however, which is not always easy for educators to accept. Often we are put in the position of persuading students to come around to the interpretive communities we condone (e.g., teaching students the interpretive practices of thinking like a historian or expecting students to sit quietly and listen). Yet resistance can be the beginning of interpretation rather than an end to the lesson (Dewey, 1916).

David Buckingham (2003) explains that resistance can be turned into an exercise in play and creativity. Students can represent their understandings of popular media through a variety of other media, such as video skits or advertisements, just as the students from the Ron Clark Academy did by their text transformation of T.I.'s lyrics into a detailed synopsis of the presidential candidates' platforms.

Buckingham (2003) argues, however, that teachers should also encourage students to examine and interpret their own creative and playful interpretations of pop culture. **Critical framing**, an extension of the critical and recontextualized instructional models (described in Chapter 2), asks students to reflect on their own and others' assigned meanings of what they have produced to get at why they chose particular images and wordings. But teachers should avoid assigning written reflections, which can seem to students like an artificial and distant way of approaching their own productions. Buckingham notes that critical framing works better when students discuss an audience's (e.g., classmates) interpretations after experiencing their work.

ADDITIONAL RESOURCES

1. **Try critical framing.** Consult the following book for more examples on how teachers have encouraged students to reflect on their own pop culture productions: *Media education: Literacy, learning and contemporary culture* (Buckingham, 2003).
2. **Students as producers.** Have students produce their own videos and post them on the Web. TeacherTube (http://www. teachertube.com/) offers an alternative to YouTube and focuses on videos made for school projects.
3. **Interpretation and popular culture.** See Richard Shusterman's website (http://www.shusterman.net/media.html) for more about interpretive practices and pop culture. Shusterman studies interpretation and pop culture. This link offers a sample of his commentaries on the importance of pop culture texts in how people engage in interpretation and understanding.

CHAPTER 5

Who Do People Think I Am, and Who Do I Want to Be?

Photo of Manning Pruden © Manning Pruden

It's like Education 101. You need to know who you are teaching. For example, not only that kids are from a certain SES [socioeconomic status] but that they listen to certain music and dress a certain way. It's not data to just say, "I've got seven black kids, seven Latinos, and this many girls and boys." It's like *what you do with it*. You don't walk into a board room completely unprepared for whom you're presenting for. You do your research on how best to present your product, your ideas, whatever you're trying to pitch. We need to know our clients. Big corporations do this. If they can do that, we can connect to our students.

—Manning Pruden, middle grades reading intervention teacher, interview

Ms. Pruden works hard to connect to her "clients." The students she teaches have difficulty demonstrating proficiency in traditional print-based reading. She says her students are frustrated, disengaged, and "ready to quit it all." She knows they care and want to succeed in school, but

Ms. Pruden has undergraduate degrees in studio art and middle school education. She has been a middle school literacy coach and reading intervention teacher in the United States and has taught middle/high school in South Africa.

they don't like the stigma that comes with needing assistance. "They come into class with their pants hanging down and hoodies over their eyes. The boys slouch low in their seats, and the girls put their heads on their desks. Really, they would rather be thought of as bad asses than dumb asses," she explained. How can a **"pop culture pedagogy"** (Jabari, 2001) help us connect to the students we teach?

*A **pop culture pedagogy** refers to people's pop culture text choices that reveal personal identification and meaning-making. Studying text choices and text uses illustrates how adolescents use pop culture to inform their identities and their literacy practices.*

HOW DO WE USE POP CULTURE TO CONSTRUCT IDENTITY?

Audiences continuously negotiate meanings of pop culture texts. As everyday culture, pop culture is always contested. As we discussed in Chapter 1, the producer's assigned meaning of text might differ from the audiences' constructed and accepted meaning. Therefore, texts are always up for audience interpretation (see Chapters 3 and 4). And audiences use pop culture to construct meanings and desired identities. Take, for example, the following discussion presented by Ms. Pruden.

For several days, two 6th-grade girls cut one another off in class when speaking by "giving the Heisman." They turned their

See www.heisman.com for a description and pictures of the Heisman Award.

face and a shoulder away from one another and pulled one hand into their chest while placing the other "stiff arm" in the speaker's face. This gesture is reminiscent of the stance depicted on the Heisman trophy, the prestigious college football award.

I knew these girls had little interest in sports, much less college football, and I asked what they were doing.

They replied, "Giving the Heisman."

I asked, "What does it mean to give the Heisman?"

"It's like tellin' someone to shut up or that you don't wanna talk to them no more."

"So, it's like giving someone 'the hand'?" I asked.

They quickly let me know that it was like that, but "not so old."

They said, "It comes from a song. We learned it from the music video." Then they showed me the moves. (They hesitated to give me the name of the song because it is called "Do Da Heisman on Dat Hoe" by the Dem Heizman Boyz [2002].)

> See *http://www.metrolyrics.com/do-da-heisman-lyrics-dem-heizman-boyz.html* for the lyrics to this song.

I asked, "Do you know where the term *Heisman* originated?"

They said, "I just thought it was a move for the song. What is it?"

I told them the history of the Heisman as best I could, due to my lack of interest in college football. We discussed how the Heisman depicted in the music video is similar to the move on the football field. In both instances, it is used to hold off a person or to stop them from going forward.

Students often surprise me with the usage of a word or action they create from their pop culture interests but have a limited understanding of its other uses in other contexts.

—Mrs. Pruden, personal reflection

The assigned and accepted meanings of "the Heisman" morphs from context to context depending on the audience's text uses to construct identity. The girls learned about "the Heisman" not from an attachment to football or from knowledge of the coveted collegiate trophy, but from a rap song. Yet they did not use the assigned meanings of identity given by the heterosexual male rappers. Instead, the girls interpreted the text to match their own female identities to communicate with each other within a context of friendship.

We can infer audiences' identities by the texts they choose to represent themselves. But, as described in Chapter 4, interpretations don't always match up. In everyday culture, the text producer (author) and the audience have some control over the uses of texts for creating identities. Audiences both take on a text's assigned meanings of representations of identities (such as race, class, gender, age, ability, and ethnicity), and construct their own accepted meanings dependent on their interpretive communities, their beliefs, and their social networks. Table 5.1 summarizes how production-in-use functions for audiences.

Table 5.1. Production-in-Use: Audiences' Use of Identity and Subjectivity

Authorial intent yields assigned meaning and identities	*Audiences' uses yield both accepted meaning and constructed meaning*
• What is the author's assigned meaning for using a particular picture, character, icon, or wording? • How does the author portray particular identities (such as age, race, gender, class, and ability) in the text? • Do I agree with the meaning the author assigned to the identity?	• What use do I have for this text? • How will I shape this text to meet my needs? • How do I want to use this text to create meaning within my own social networks? • How can this text help me construct meaning to forward my ideas and to represent myself?
Authors create **identities** when they assign meaning to a text. Audiences can accept the assigned meaning, or they can construct their own (see right column).	Audiences use **subjectivity**—the unstable, shifting self that keeps text use and meaning in motion—when they reject a text's assigned meaning and construct their own.

IDENTITY AND SUBJECTIVITY PLAYED OUT

The following excerpts from Timony's production-in-use illustrates the nuanced working of identity and subjectivity when using pop culture. How might you have approached Timony as one of your students?

Timony's self-chosen pseudonym came from reading Heavier Than Heaven *(Cross, 2002), a biography of Kurt Cobain. In the book, Timony found an obscure reference to a Cobain tribute song from Napster.com entitled "I Love You Anyway." Simon Fair Timony, a 10-year-old boy, composed the song. Timony wrote Margaret in an email, "It's a (excuse me, but for lack of a better word) cute song!!!!" (Hagood, 2002, p. 250)*

Timony was a bright 8th grader and a voracious reader. But his teachers speculated that he "might be in some way disturbed." They were concerned about his clothing choices. He often wore his favorite black T-shirt stating "I hear voices and they don't like you!" in bold white letters across his chest. He also donned dark-colored tees with a silkscreen print of Nirvana playing grunge music in a Seattle bar or a close-up of Cobain, with his eyes wide and screaming mouth open. Sometimes when he played his trombone in band class, he'd amuse his friends by contorting his torso, making Kurt Cobain's mouth move as if singing. His teachers read these shirts as texts that expressed a troubling aspect of Timony's identity. His math teacher commented, "He is in a typical sort of rebellion pattern or whatever against society, and I know that the Columbine thing scared everybody." And his language arts teacher ruminated, "In the wake of Columbine, we have to be aware of kids like Timony."

One day, Timony's friend Alex was playing with a guitar pick in math class, chewing it like gum. When the teacher asked what was in his mouth, Timony threw his hands in the air and yelled, "No! It's a weapon! UUGGH! Careful! Careful! Alex has a weapon!" The teacher stood quickly, asking, "What is it?" Alex and Timony began to laugh. The teacher looked sternly at Timony and gave him a silent lunch (a punishment whereby he had to eat lunch silently in a room separate from the cafeteria) for "disruptive behavior," which later resulted in time spent in ISS [in-school suspension]. (Hagood, 2002)

How do Timony's pop culture choices, from Nirvana T-shirts to his references to "it's a weapon" (evoking media images of school violence), assign meaning and produce his identity? How does Timony subjectively create different meaning from the texts in different contexts, compared to how his teachers read the texts, and their authorial intentions? How does a guitar pick become a weapon? How do these pop culture texts function as everyday culture?

Reflection Activity: Rewind and Redo?

Knobel (1999) reminds us that students "will benefit most from an approach to language education that engages them in investigating how language is a social practice, and how meanings along with their own social identities and subjectivities are socially constituted" (p. 222).

- How might teachers' perceptions of Timony have changed if they had embraced a pop culture pedagogy for learning about his pop culture interests and his identities and subjectivities?
- What might have happened if the teacher had analyzed Timony's production-in-use, both to accept certain meanings and identities (a troubled adolescent) and to construct new subjectivities that resist those assigned identities?
- How might the teacher/student relationship have changed, and how might this change have informed the teaching of content by allowing the teacher to connect it to pop culture?
- How might the instructional content have changed had the teacher/student relationship been different?
- What recommendations might you give Timony's teachers based on a view of pop culture as everyday culture?

CHALLENGES TO CREATING A COMMUNITY OF TRUST

Excellent instruction is built on creating a community of trust. Community building includes learning about students' lives, which involves a lot of pop culture, and then connecting those interests to instruction. Trust building takes time, and time is a scarce commodity in schools.

Finding Time to Talk Pop Culture

Time isn't built into the curriculum for respecting and learning about students' pop culture interests. Speaking to this challenge in an interview, Ms. Pruden said:

> You are trying to break a trend that's been going on forever of differences between out-of-school and in-school tensions. So you're showing up one day and trying to do this and think that you're in [with students]? You're not. It doesn't work that way. It takes time. Pop culture is a culture, and culture is developed over time.

Beyond the activities presented in Chapter 1, how can you learn about students' interests in authentic and efficient ways?

> *Reflecting on the formation of adolescents' reading identities, Alvermann (2001) explained that "cultures are the ways of 'doing' life, not simply products of that life." (p. 678)*

Dispelling Movie Myths

Contentious teacher and student identities are popular tropes in representations of schooling. Take, for example, the teacher/student relationships depicted in two box office movie hits. LouAnne Johnson, the marine-turned-teacher is portrayed in the biographical account in *Dangerous Minds* (Bass, 1995). Her racially, ethnically, and socioeconomically diverse students dubbed her "white bread." The story of Erin Gruwell and a class of 9th-grade students who work together and learn about one another through writing diaries in *Freedom Writers* (LaGravenese, 2007) presents a similar tale. In these films (and in their book counterparts), conflicts between the students' and teachers' identities are palpable. These women's efforts to connect with students are thwarted and ignored until heated arguments about identities—

> *The scene in* Dangerous Minds *when the teacher and students discuss Bob Dylan's lyrics and Dylan Thomas's poetry illustrates the tensions in reading and identities.*
> *The movie trailer at www.freedomwriters.com alludes to some of the identity conflicts in* Freedom Writers.

of both teacher and student interpretations of the other, some of which are related to both groups' pop culture interests—surface.

These texts situate teachers and students in oppositional identities, with their values, beliefs and understandings about pop culture in conflict. How could they be used to create a conversation in a classroom?

Reflection Activity: Representations of Teacher Identities in Popular Culture

- Watch a popular film in which your profession is portrayed. Take a look at http://www.oswego.edu/~beyerbac/representations_of_teachers_in_6.html for a list of films about representation of adults and adolescents in educational settings.
- What stereotypical identities of teacher, media specialist, literacy coach, or administrator are put forth?
- How does this assigned meaning of identity compare to the assumptions and beliefs about your self-created identity as an educator and about your own pop culture interests?
- Why do you think this text became popular?
- Have adolescents view the same text and examine how student identities are represented in relation to pop culture and to teacher identities.
- If you and your students were to rewrite the text, what identities would you assign to teacher and student characters?

CONNECTING STUDENT IDENTITY, TEACHER IDENTITY, AND INSTRUCTION

Adults, too, need to include and share their pop culture interests. Doing so opens up opportunities to study similarities and differences of text interests and uses with students. Adults and adolescents learn to respect one another's interests and to understand the value and pleasures placed on text (Xu, 2004). Sharing also acknowledges the power of both teachers and students to create meaning and uses for texts, assisting in the building of a collaborative community of trust.

Ms. Pruden understands that for teachers to grab hold of adolescents' pop culture to include it in their instruction can be jarring for some students who are used to having their pop culture ignored, excluded, or even ridiculed by some educators in school. It is also a one-sided approach:

You have to pay your dues as a teacher and prove that you have some pop culture clout. It can't be a gimmick. Kids more than anyone will know if you're genuine about it. A lot of teachers use it, but when they're using it, they're making fun of it. Even if I just toss out something like "Getting Silly With It" (a popular rap song), it might not fly. But if I actually have a conversation and prove that I respect what they value and not just show off with one tidbit of pop culture, then I can get a genuine response and students' respect. That's a big deal. Why should kids trust and respect what we have to offer if we don't respect their pop culture? (Ms. Pruden, interview)

> *Ms. Pruden's pop culture interests: I hate reality TV because it's scripted, not reality. But I like scripted drama, like CSI and House. I have eclectic music interests. I might listen to Red Hot Chili Peppers, Kerry Underwood, Lil Boosie, or Ryan Adams. I like music where I can hear the lyrics and pronounce the words. I like Christian music sometimes. It sort of depends on where I am.*

Pop Culture in Action: Adolescents' Readings of Identities in Media

Joan Hilton co-teaches with Ms. Pruden in a 6th-grade English/language arts class in a public middle school serving a diverse socioeconomic population in Charleston.

The following 3-day lesson plan focuses on the relationship between popular television shows and student identity. The teachers used the term *media* (rather than *text*) to describe various multimodalities (radio, television, film). The mini-unit was part of a larger study on propaganda. The teachers adapted their lesson plans from a lesson they found on critical media literacy (see http://www.readwritethink.org/lessons/lesson_view.asp?id=96).

> *As a wife and mother of two high-schoolers, I encounter pop culture everyday, especially through music. For example, YouTube videos help fellow choir members and me develop the dynamics needed for a better performance. And my daughters frequently download new music in my iPod in order to "broaden" my musical experience.—Joan Hilton, 6th-grade teacher, interview*

> *English/language arts standards addressed:*
> - *Analyze central ideas within and across informational texts*
> - *Draw conclusions and make inferences*
> - *Interpret information from graphic features*
> - *Write for a specific audience.*

Day 1

Objective: Define *media* and analyze student media interests by categories (gender, age, race, etc.).

1. Students define *media*. Prompt ideas until they understand that *media* refers to various means of communication. Give examples from television, radio, and the newspaper.
2. Students write facts about themselves for 1 minute. Prompt with: gender, race, age, interests, looks, personality, sports, and religion.

3. Students categorize identities into "where I can find myself in the media" and "where I cannot find myself in the media." Discuss.
4. Students complete Pop Culture Survey (see Table 1.1). Finish for homework if necessary.
5. Students read "A Different World: Children's Perceptions of Race and Class in Media" (see http://www.media-awareness.ca/english/resources/research_documents/reports/diversity/different_world.cfm).
6. Questions to consider during reading:
    a. When a class or race of people is presented in the media positively, are they valued?
    b. When a class or race of people is presented in the media negatively, are they not valued?
    c. Describe how minority characters are stereotyped in the media.
    d. Which groups of people are portrayed positively and negatively in the news?

    Homework: Students watch a 30-minute teen sitcom or drama and complete a media observation sheet (see http://www.readwritethink.org/lesson_images/lesson96/media_ob.pdf).

Day 2

Objectives: Discover how popular culture interests help shape identities. Students critically view and analyze media's representations of identities.

1. Revisit where students find characters like themselves in popular culture. Record student responses on chart paper.
2. Discuss television shows viewed for homework. Questions to consider:
    a. Why was the show created? Was the purpose more than entertainment? Was the writer/producer/television station making a deeper statement?
    b. How were the characters' identities represented? Negatively? Positively? Both? Why? How did these representations make you feel while watching? Were you uncomfortable? If so, why?
    c. Did you feel differently if the characters were live actors or animated characters?

3. Determine whether media imitate life. Does the portrayal of groups of people in the media shape their identities? Why or why not?
   a. Students define *stereotyping*.
   b. Do the media keep up with changing society? Compare and contrast television today with the 1950s.

Day 3

Objective: Create an informational piece that describes your popular culture identity.

1. Ask students if they have a MySpace or Facebook account.
   a. Discuss backgrounds and information they include and how they identify with their choices.
   b. Ask if their friends include information that does not reflect the identities they know about the person. Discuss why they might create different identities.
   c. Review Internet safety and the importance of considering representation.
2. View sample profile pages. Have students attempt to identify by age, race, and gender. Discuss how they can infer that information based on profile descriptions.
3. Discuss items typically found on a Web profile. Create a layout as a model.
4. Have students create a Web profile based on their popular culture interests and on their thinking about media's representations of people.

Ms. Hilton's and Ms. Pruden's instruction revealed much about young adolescents' interests. Ms. Hilton commented:

> It is refreshing to see how far the typical adolescent/teenager has come in 10 years regarding tolerance and diversity. While most see negative portrayal of race in the media, they do not use that to shape their beliefs or identities. When asked why a writer of a television program would put down certain classes, races, or genders of people in a script, most students had no answer. (personal reflection)

Similarly, Ms. Pruden said that students "easily located stereotypes and made astute observations of media's negative representations of race." For example, Matthew noted in his reflection on shows that portray races negatively: "like the comedy show *Nail Salon,* where this half-White half-Asian boy goes into a nail store called Beautiful Nail and starts talking different and picking on the Chinese girls working in there." (Ms. Pruden asked, "How did he talk differently?") "Like saying things like 'whach yoou whant we doo fo you.'" (Ms. Pruden asked, "How does this portray Asians?") Matthew responded, "That they talk funny and their voice is squeaky and stuff and that they work in nail places and building buildings."

Ms. Hilton and Ms. Pruden found that students understood the connections between genre (such as comedy) and exaggerated characterizations. Students also understood the technique of parody that television programs employ to represent various identities, often negatively. Students identified how shows often assigned particular stereotypical identities, but they did not necessarily accept the meaning of those identities fully. This finding isn't surprising. Other media educators have documented that students don't mindlessly accept the stereotyping and negative images of that media assigned to identities (Cohen, 1998; Funge, 1998).

ADDITIONAL RESOURCES

1. **View the video "Merchants of Cool" to examine the symbiotic intertwinings of adolescents and the media.** See (www.pbs.org/wgbh/pages/frontline/shows/cool/view/). Discuss with a group of colleagues your thoughts on the portrayal of production-in-use. Specifically note the ways in which media assign identities that adolescents accept and how media reflect adolescents' identities learned about through studying their own uses of pop culture.

2. **Examine portrayals of teacher and student identities in pop culture in** *Education in Popular Culture: Telling Tales on Teachers and Learners* (Fisher, Harris, & Jarvis, 2008). Then, analyze how adults and young people are portrayed in the movies and identify issues of representation related to sexuality, bullying, race, and gender.

3. **Do you use social networking sites, such as Facebook, MySpace, LinkedIn, or Ning?** If so, how do you use them? For what purposes? Or have you been invited to join, but not done so? Check out these sites and compare them. Make a list of pros and cons of using them to connect with students.

CHAPTER 6

Conclusions: Connecting Across Generations via Turning Around Pedagogies

Connecting to the Next Generation

Student Z day dreamily drums his desk
Is this his subconscious form of protest?
To the paper and pencil and reading at his seat
The areas of learning he feels he can't compete.

That poetry unit I put off to the last minute
Student Z is alive and "all up in it"
He actually hurries to class and is on time
He loves playing with words and making them rhyme

In a lesson on homographs Student X played around
With the words that he read and their interesting sound
The musical sound that words can create
Are lost to a child labeled nonreader as his fate.

I have to rethink how I plan and teach
How do I get to the ones out of reach?
More imaginative writing should I allow
Overlooking conventions without a raised brow?

This culture of Hip-Hop can have both con and pro
It brings out creativity that test scores don't show
This pleasure, this immersion, this engaging, this rap
May actually be a strategy to "cover" the testing crap!

A paradigm shift this old teacher needs to make
It may help Student Z and X stay awake
A love for the thing should be my ultimate goal
To connect reading and writing to a student's soul.
    —Leslie Barrett-Jones, post to an online course discussion board

Ms. Barrett-Jones was a 6th-grade language arts/reading and social studies teacher when she posted her poem in an online course.
Later, after completing an Education Specialist degree in reading,
she became a high school reading specialist/literacy coach. She
closed an email to Donna by noting that while she has been teaching for 24 years, she is "still changing :>."

Ms. Barrett-Jones's poem encapsulates a semester's worth of reflecting on her in-school tutoring of a boy (referred to variously as
Student Z and X). For several consecutive years, he experienced difficulty with the reading portion of the state's criterion-referenced
competency test. He had to retake the statewide 5th-grade reading test to qualify for promotion. The boy's perception of himself
as a reader was not good; in fact, that was one of the reasons Ms.
Barrett-Jones decided to work with him. She "turned around" her
pedagogy to find ways to engage his interest in pop culture rather
than assume he would come around to her usual way of teaching
language arts.

Ms. Barrett-Jones wants to connect to the next generation. In this
concluding chapter, we focus on connecting teachers and students
by connecting pop culture texts and texts that connect to instruction. We don't believe that teachers, school media specialists, librar-

ians, and administrators should integrate pop culture into literacy learning for the purpose of *teaching* pop culture in schools or as a hook to grab students' attention only to move on to more relevant and "real" academic texts. Boxing in either pop culture or instruction as though they were opposites—or as if one were subservient to the other—misses the connections within and across both. To create the paradigm shift, Ms. Barrett-Jones alludes to requires **turn-around pedagogies** (Comber & Kamler, 2005), a concept introduced later in the chapter.

CONNECTING ACROSS GENERATIONS

Schools signal their stance on the use of pop culture in classrooms, libraries, and media centers in numerous ways, some of which carry more clout than others. The outcome, however, is pretty much the same: Adults are placed in the role of watchful guardians responsible for protecting students from real or imagined harm; students are viewed as naive or needing to remember "they're in school"—a rationale thought to end all ifs, ands, or buts. Case settled; settled that is, until the bell for changing classes rings or, in the lower grades, it's time to line up, "pull out their 12-inch voices" (er, whispers), and wait. Students and adults are positioned (and at times position themselves) as being in full-fledged opposition to one another. Why is this so?

Gee (1996) claims that when people engage in constructing and sustaining certain ways of being in relation to some other person or phenomenon—say, pop culture—they communicate through speech, actions, dress, music, magazines, and myriad other ways what it takes to recognize themselves, and be recognized by others, as belonging to a particular group. They do this by donning what Gee refers to as **identity kits**, a concept related to interpretive communities because identity kits can shape how people interpret texts. Timony (in Chapter 5) is a good example of this conduct. Identity kits serve the useful (or, we would claim, not so useful) function of separating the adults from the students in terms of pop culture use in schools.

This book encourages teachers to push against labels that would confine adults and students to hard-and-fast categories as though there were few, if any, shared commonalities and interests across generations. We resist attempts to polarize "them" and "us":

[D]efining the Millennial Generation as youth who solely spend their time mindlessly and acritically playing with computers, video games, and music [runs] the risk of dismissing the highly engaging and increasingly valid literacies they create in their engagement with various media. And, to assume that adults have little or no desire to learn about diverse literacies created in the last ten years shortchanges them as well. (Hagood, Stevens, & Reinking, 2002, p. 79)

Teachers' and students' pop culture interests often overlap (as in the discussion about the affinity for rap in Chapter 3). But the identity kits for being a teacher and being a student set up oppositional views of pop culture that perpetuate the notion of stereotypical identities.

MAKING A SPACE FOR LEARNING WITH 21ST-CENTURY TEXTS IN SCHOOLS

As discussed in Chapter 3, having an appreciative audience motivates adolescents to author texts (Alvermann, 2008) or join social networking sites (as illustrated in the Introduction). Having a place to demonstrate skills in using 21st-century texts was of key importance in a study of 4000 6th-, 7th-, and 8th-grade students in North Carolina who participated in a statewide after-school program (Spires, Lee, Turner, & Johnson, 2008). Based on data collected from surveys and focus-group interviews, Spires and her colleagues reported that students wanted the successes they were experiencing in the after-school program recognized and appreciated *in* school. For that to happen, school leaders may want to consider the benefits of working collaboratively with youth to bring about what Morrell (2008) describes as "collective action for social change" (p. 137). For example, principals, teachers, and community groups might engage with young people in drawing up plans for incorporating school-wide some of the programmatic highlights in the North Carolina after-school program. Collective action for social change also demonstrates how literacy learning extends beyond schooled literacy practices and how a recontextualized instructional model (see Chapter 2) positively impacts students' and teachers' literacy learning.

Orchestrating connections between schooled literacy and students' interests in 21st-century texts may seem overwhelming (or even off-putting) at first, but this need not remain the case. Starting small and taking baby steps can practically assure success. We offer a few suggestions for stepping out, but first it's time to take stock of what's in your backpack to see if it needs repacking before taking those initial steps.

In this book's introduction, Genevieve's backpack overflowed with 21st-century and pop culture texts. Some required her to read print; others required her to interpret images, symbols, icons, sounds, and gestures—sometimes separately but more often in combination with other communicative modes (including print). If your backpack contains texts similar to Genevieve's, you may have little repacking to do. If not, now is the time to take stock of what's missing so that the contents of your backpack more closely resemble those of your students.

TAKING STOCK

Are the changes associated with 21st-century texts and literacy learning making themselves visible with such speed and intensity that what we once viewed as a possibility is now a fact (or even after the fact)? Dawn Hogue (2008), a teacher from Sheboygan Falls High School, suggests the latter. Ms. Hogue reminded her audience at the 2008 Wisconsin State Reading Association that time waits for no one, especially for literacy educators in these current times. In fact, using the

> *Margaret attended a talk Ron Clark gave about strategies for invigorating the curriculum. He recounted the story behind the video "You Can Vote However You Like" (Chapter 1). A teacher observing at Ron Clark Academy made a video on her cell phone of students performing the rap. She later posted it to YouTube (unbeknownst to the school). Several days later (after the video had reached 25,000 hits), Clark received a phone call with a request for the lyrics from another school. Initially unaware of what the caller was talking about, he later watched the video, which climbed from 25,000 hits to 1 million in just 3 days. This example of pop culture as everyday culture—and its morphing into a CNN special—is reflective of the speed and intensity of the dissemination of 21st-century texts.*

past tense to drive home her message, Hogue summed up the state of affairs in less than a dozen words: "Keyboards changed how we write. The Internet changed how we communicate" (n. p.). Indeed. We would add that the Internet is producing changes in its own right. For example, as shown in Table 6.1, differences exist in thinking and working styles between a Web 1.0 and 2.0 world.

To get a sense of what's different in the two worlds, look at Table 6.1 and see if you can find patterns in the differences. One distinguishing characteristic is that collaboration, user-produced content, and user-disseminated content are more prevalent in a Web 2.0 world than in a Web 1.0 world. On a personal note, what beliefs about 21st-century texts do you hold that allow you to function in one world better than the other or in both worlds simultaneously? How does your view of pop culture affect how you approach each of these worlds?

Table 6.1. Differences in Web 1.0 and Web 2.0

Web 1.0	Web 2.0
Ofoto	Flickr
Britannica Online	Wikipedia
Personal websites (static, more control)	Blogging (interactive, less control)
Publisher has the expertise	Participants share expertise
Content management systems	Wikis
Directories (top-down taxonomies)	Tagging (bottom-up classification)
Netscape (software products)	Google (a service, not products)

Source: Adapted from Knobel & Lankshear [2007] p. 16. Used by permission of publisher.

Reflection Activity: Time to Repack?

Find your copy of Table Int.4, "Analysis of Your Textual Day in a Life." Examine your textual artifacts in light of your answer to this question: What beliefs about 21st-century texts do you hold that allow you to function in a Web 1.0 world more easily than a Web 2.0 world (or vice versa), or in both worlds simultaneously? Remember, you are trying to figure out the small steps you need to take in order to help students make connections between schooled literacy and their interests in 21st-century texts. The following questions probe how much (if any) repacking you need to do:

- Are there items in your backpack that you need to keep? Why?
- Do you need to remove some items? Which ones?
- What do you need to add to your backpack?
- What items need shifting over for a more comfortable fit?

TURN-AROUND PEDAGOGIES

We've learned a great deal from the teachers and library media specialists who shared their work with us and opened our eyes to the substantive learning and teaching that occurs when we connect students' interests in pop culture texts to the school curriculum. Their pedagogies will inform our own as we continue to explore possibilities for engaging others in this exciting work.

What Are Turn-Around Pedagogies?

"Turn-around pedagogies" is a term that Barbara Comber and Barbara Kamler (2005) coined to describe the impact of five teams of teachers' redesigns of their literacy programs over a 3-year span.

Contesting the **deficit assumptions** that can hold back both teachers and students in their efforts to learn, Comber and Kamler used the term to evoke images of "the kind of pedagogic, curriculum and people work required for connecting and reconnecting students with literacy" (p. 7). We use it here to describe the kind of work that Ms. Barrett-Jones was doing when she reflected in her poem on needing to change her pedagogic approach to literacy instruction if she hoped to connect with Student Z/X's interests in pop culture.

A useful term, *turn-around pedagogies* also reflects Ms. Dabit's instruction (see Chapter 2) in her 8th-grade reading class when she changed from teaching "Paul Revere's Ride" in her usual way (read, reread, and answer teacher-posed questions) to incorporating her students' interests in pop culture texts. Using students' responses on the Pop Culture Survey (see Table 1.1) to guide her, Ms. Dabit linked their interest in movies, graphic novels and manga, and MapQuest to a famous figure in the New England colonists' bid for freedom.

Similarly, in Chapter 1, Ms. Cowan tapped into resources she had available as a school library media specialist to address a question one of her 4th-grade students asked as he checked out Mary Shelley's *Frankenstein*: "You [Ms. Cowan] have some pretty good books in here, but why don't you have *Star Wars*?" Spurred into action by this boy's query, Ms. Cowan beefed up the library collection. She also set up a schoolwide blog that resulted in online social networking around books. Students and teachers blogged feverishly about their favorite books, and circulation in the school library rose noticeably.

Not only experienced teachers and school library media specialists practiced turn-around pedagogies. In Chapter 4, we saw how Ms. Wuerfel, a prospective teacher, enlisted her children and their friends in designing a lesson that included their favorite lyrics. Learning about the relevance of interpretive communities through multiple representations of the lyrics in their repertoire was likely an experience that they'll not soon forget. A lesson we can take from Ms. Wuerfel's planning is that trusting students to bring their skills in using multimodal pop culture texts to bear on curricular tasks is easy for them and a boon to busy teachers who might otherwise need some "coaching" on the side.

What Else Do Turn-Around Pedagogies Promise?

In previous chapters, we've witnessed a hit parade of effective practices showing how turn-around pedagogies can enliven teaching and learning. What else do they bring to our professional

"So, there I was, tied to an altar made from outdated encyclopedias, about to get sacrificed to the dark powers by a cult of evil Librarians." —Alcatraz Smedry in Alcatraz Versus the Evil Librarians *(Sanderson, 2007).*

lives? For one, they are essential to changing the larger, schoolwide/culturewide paradigm shift that Ms. Barrett-Jones alludes to in the last stanza of "Connecting to the Next Generation." How do they do this? Pedagogies that turn us around as educators stand to do the same thing for students.

For example, the students who participated in Mr. Cooper's social studies lesson that involved examining multiple pop culture texts to learn about critical reading had the opportunity to get excited about something that, given a different set of texts, they might have viewed as mundane and irrelevant (see Chapter 4). As such, turn-around pedagogies can create learning conditions that push against students viewing teachers and school library media specialists as simply "pop-up" educators ready to go through the motions that satisfied a definition of teaching in the past. Teaching in the 21st-century— when attention, not information, is in scarce supply—can make all of us feel at times like the pop-ups on our computer screens—the ones that students know all too well how to make disappear.

SO HOW DO WE BRING ON THIS TURNING AROUND?

There is a growing body of research in literacy education (e.g., Beach & O'Brien, 2008; Marsh, 2008) that provides information on how turn-around pedagogies can support a school culture in which teachers and library media specialists can begin to integrate pop culture texts into the curriculum. Key elements summarized from this research appear in Table 6.2. Think about using this information as a bare-bones approach to understanding what your school culture supports presently and which elements are emerging. Likewise, which elements are missing but could be brought along? Who are the movers and shakers in your school, in the community, in professional organizations to which you belong who might be part of a support network? Don't overlook the technology support services that your district and/or local businesses might provide.

Information gleaned from the research literature in the second column of Table 6.2 appears in the form of strategies for interpreting and producing pop culture texts. Be strategic in demonstrating to colleagues, building, and district-level administrators, as well as parents, that you understand pop culture texts are not merely for consumption; they are also produced by students—daughters and sons, and future community leaders who will likely have jobs and careers fueled by 21st-century texts and literacies yet to be named.

Table 6.2. Bringing on the Paradigm Shift Through Turn-Around Pedagogies

Factors affecting successful integration of pop culture texts with instruction (adapted from Marsh, 2008)	*Strategies for interpreting and producing pop culture texts (adapted from Beach & O'Brien, 2008)*
• Building on students' interests • Communicating with administrators and parents • Supporting networks of stakeholders (teachers, school library media specialists, students, administrators, families, professional organizations) • Sustaining turn-around pedagogies over time • Including multiple modes and media	• Linking knowledge construction to pop culture texts, standards, and the curriculum • Constructing identities • Linking, connecting, and revising texts • Interpreting and using genre features • Searching for and organizing text material based on critical inquiry • Critiquing popular culture texts

---

Reflection Activity:
Strategies for Small Steps

Take a few minutes to consider what small steps are necessary for this work to occur in your own school. Remember: The turn-around pedagogies project that Comber and Kamler (2005) initiated took 3 years to achieve. Reassess once again what's in your *repacked* backpack (Table I.4) and make a list of the strategies from Table 6.2 that might assist you in taking the small steps necessary for achieving your own turn-around pedagogy. Consider your goals and objectives for including turn-around pedagogies in year 1, 2, and 3. Also, discuss this plan with students. What are their suggestions and critiques?

LAST WORDS

If implementing turn-around pedagogies in the school where you work still seems a bit daunting at this point, take heart. We live in a world where we can open our cell phones faster than we can open a letter, where authoring ideas and texts need not be a solitary or a completely original enterprise. How we make sense of all this, and who we invite as co-backpackers, will make a world of difference in the way we connect across generations. Pop culture can serve as conduits through which we reach out for such connections; turn-around pedagogies can extend that reach. Both hold promise for teaching and learning to meet the 21st-century literacy learning demands of working with multimodal and intertextual texts that include pop culture.

ADDITIONAL RESOURCES

1. **Notice how Kinga Varga-Dobai's (2008) analysis of a young reader's use of pop culture transforms Aesop's classic fable "The Crow and the Pitcher" into a more meaningful text.** The original fable tells how a thirsty crow unable to drink from a deep pitcher half-filled with water drops pebbles into the pitcher, causing the water to rise and thus become accessible for drinking. In the revised version, a horse and narrow bowl replace the crow and pitcher. Gatorade and gum balls replace the water and pebbles. Think of other examples that show how people throughout history have made literature more relevant for themselves.

2. **Do you know students who enjoy playing with the sounds and meanings of homophones, as Ms. Barrett-Jones' student did?** If so, check out wordplay books like Terban's (2008) *The Dove Dove*. We found over 500 similar titles at http://www. amazon.com. Choose five titles that you might use and give a rationale for why you selected each.

3. **Read Kathy Sanford's (2008) *Video Games in the Library? What Is The World Coming To?* to garner support for using 21-st century and pop culture texts in your school.** Sanford's article focuses on ways school librarians support classroom learning through new technologies and texts. List the steps you would take to put this turn-around pedagogy in place.

Glossary

Accepted meaning—an audience consumer's interpretation of a text (see *Production-in-use*).

Anime—short for Japanese animation. Characters are distinctive and usually depicted with exaggerated physical features such as large heads, doe-shaped eyes, big hair, and long bodies.

Artifacts—texts that show users' identities, values, beliefs, and literacy learning in their social practices of connecting to others through text choices.

Assigned meaning—a text producer's intended meaning of a text (see *Production-in-use*).

Blog—shorthand for a *Web log* that invites online interactions around multimodal texts ranging from news commentary to personal diaries, graphics, and videos.

Construct meaning—users determine how they will use a text in a given context and decide what the text means.

Critical awareness—the explicit questioning of how texts are produced and consumed.

Critical consciousness—the recognition that while economic, social, and political injustices exist in society, people are capable of taking actions against these oppressions.

Critical framing—activity in which students reflect on their own and others' assigned meanings of what they have produced to get at why they chose particular images and wordings.

Deficit assumptions—misdirected beliefs that students have little if anything to contribute to their own learning.

Everyday culture—one view of pop culture that assumes that both text producers and audiences hold meaning-making potential. The study of texts focuses on the producer's intended meaning and on the audiences' constructed meaning, which may differ.

Fan fiction—stories that fans of an original work (e.g., *Harry Potter* series) write by changing the settings, characters, and plot of the original to create different scenes and situations across genres and media.

Folk culture—one view of pop culture that assumes that texts have no inherent meaning. It focuses on audiences' constructed meaning and uses of texts.

Game literacy—writing scripts for games; researching and authoring backstories (the histories behind various game plots); producing walkthroughs (video-captured directions for playing the games).

Identity—the assigned meanings given to identity categories—such as age, race, gender, class, and ability—when authoring texts.

Identity kits—a term coined by Gee (1996) to describe the ways we construct ourselves through speech, writing, reading selections, dress, music, dance, and so on that enable us to be recognized by others like ourselves as belonging to a particular group.

Inquiry—instruction focused on a problem or question that students investigate through multiple sources (and modes) of information.

Interpretation—a process of addressing uncertainty within and across texts in order to clarify and articulate what that text means in a particular context (classroom, workplace, home, etc.).

Interpretive community—a group of people tightly connected around a set of interpretive principles, or rules, that govern how interpretation is performed and how meaning is assigned. Interpretive communities usually refer to students and teachers who work together in classrooms to intepret literature texts. We use the term more broadly to cover the interpretation of a wide range of texts (including pop culture texts) in a variety of settings, not just classrooms.

Intertextuality—how texts influence each other's meaning, either multimodally or through referencing one text in relation to another.

Literacy learning—the formal and informal acquisition of communicative tools for reading, writing, listening, speaking, viewing, and designing 21st-century texts.

Literacy of fusion—a transformative pedagogy whereby teachers make deliberate use of students' interests and meld disparate elements of school-based learning and students' pop culture such that both elements make important contributions to the other's development.

Manga—the graphic counterpart of Japanese anime. Like anime, manga are more than cartoons; they include an array of texts (e.g., science fiction, cyberpunk, quasi-historical, and informational) that are read from right to left.

Mashups—technically speaking, these are hybrid Web applications, such as Google maps that combine Web-based data sources with interactive cartography; however, used in this book to refer to hybrid texts of any kind, such as remixes that include music videos, images from film or real life, print texts, and so on.

Mass culture—one view of pop culture that assumes that pop culture texts are part of low culture and unworthy of study. Audiences are thought to mindlessly accept producer's intended meanings of texts.

Multimodality—a combination of two or more modes for communicating (e.g., oral or written language, visualization, sounds, icons, gestures, performances).

Multimodal texts—messages whose meanings are open to interpretation and negotiation using a combination of two or more communicative modes (e.g., oral or written language, visualization, sounds, icons, gestures, performances).

New Criticism—a mid-20th century movement in American literary criticism defined by attention to the language devices unique to literature. Interpretation involves deriving meaning from how an author or poet uses figurative language and other literary devices, such as irony, to convey particular themes.

Pop culture pedagogy—term coined by Jabari (2001) that refers to people's pop culture text choices that reveal personal identification and meaning making.

Pop culture texts—mass-generated print and nonprint texts (e.g., comics, anime, TV shows, movies, videos, young adult books, music lyrics) that use multiple modes (e.g., linguistic, visual, aural, performative) to communicate an intended message.

Production-in-use—a view of popular culture as everyday culture in which both producers of texts and audience consumers have knowledge and power over a text's meaning.

Random access instruction—instruction that provides students with multiple multimodal representations of a concept—in the form of explanations, analogies, and other dimensions of critical thinking—so that they can revisit the concept from a variety of vantage points.

Scaffolding—initial or supportive steps that teachers take to enable students to work independently on a given task.

Schooled literacy practices—processes of reading, writing, listening, speaking, viewing, and designing that are explicitly taught and valued through stated content standards.

Second Life—an Internet-based virtual world where residents network socially while exchanging ideas, goods, and services.

Subjectivity—the unstable, shifting self that allows audiences to create different meanings and uses of texts in various contexts.

Text—a written, spoken, visual, or performed message that is interpretable and available for people to negotiate its meaning.

Turn-around pedagogies—a term coined by Comber and Kamler (2005) to describe the impact of teachers' long-term redesigns of instructional programs to contest deficit assumptions about teaching and learning.

21st-century texts—ubiquitous, familiar, and intuitive texts that communicate meaning in a variety of ways. They are "read," but they don't necessarily include "print." They include texts necessary for today's lifestyles (such as reading an online newsfeed of current events for a school project) and pop culture texts.

Visual literacy—the ability to evaluate, apply, understand, and create visual representations.

Classroom Resources

Adamson, A., & Jenson, V. (Directors). (2001). *Shrek!* [Film]. Hollywood, CA: Universal Studios/Pixar Animation Studios.

Alcott, L. M. (2004). *Little women*. New York: Signet Classics.

Anderson, M. T. (2004). *The game of sunken places*. New York: Scholastic.

Angelou, M. (n.d.). *Hip hop congress*. Retrieved March 11, 2009, from http://hiphopcongress.com/expression/poetry/poetry_archive_angelou.html

Bass, R. (Writer). (1995). *Dangerous minds* [Film]. Los Angeles: Walt Disney Studios.

Beecroft, S. (2007). *Beware the dark side.* London: Darling Kinsey Readers.

Brooks, G. (2006). *March*. New York: Viking.

Cross, C. (2002). *Heavier than heaven: A biography of Kurt Cobain*. New York: Hyperion.

De La Cruz, M. (2006). *Blue bloods*. New York: Hyperion.

Dem Heizman Boys. (2002). Do da Heisman on that hoe. On *Ghetto Heisman* [CD]. New York: Def Jam.

Donahue, A., & Zuiker, A. E. (Creators). *CSI (Crime Scene Investigation).* (2000). Retrieved June 12, 2009, from, http://www.imdb.com/title/tt0247082/

Elbert, S. (2007). (Writer and Co-Producer). *Charlotte's web: How do they do that?* (Available from IMDb, The Internet Movie Database available at http://www.us.imdb.de/title/tt1067695/fullcredits#cast

Emmerich, R. (Director). (2000). *The patriot* [Film]. Los Angeles: Sony Pictures.

Fort Minor. (2005). Kenji. On *Rising tied* [CD]. Burbank, CA: Warner Brothers Records.

Grant, J. (2002). *Frankenstein: From the story by Mary Shelley.* London: Usborne Publishing, Ltd.

Hill, F. (2000). The way you love me. On *Breathe* [CD]. Nashville: Warner Bros.

Hughes, L. (1995). Dream deferred. In A. Ranpersad (Ed.), *The collected poems of Langston Hughes*. New York: Vintage.

LaGravenese, R. (Director). (2007). *Freedom writers* [Film]. Los Angeles: Paramount.

Lewis, C. S. (1950). *The lion, the witch, and the wardrobe.* Bel Air, CA: Geoffrey Bles.

Meyer, S. (2005). *Twilight.* New York: Little, Brown.

Myracle, L. (2007). *L8r, g8r.* New York: Amulet Books.

Olson, N. (2006). *Nathan Hale: Revolutionary spy.* Mankato, MN: Capstone Press.

Pink Floyd. (1979). Another brick in the wall: Part I. On *The wall* [CD]. Chicago: Mobile Fidelity.

Rowling, J. K. (2002). *Harry Potter and the chamber of secrets.* New York: Scholastic.

Sachar, L. (1998). *Holes.* New York: Farrar, Straus & Girouux.

Sanderson, B. (2007). *Alcatraz versus the evil librarians.* New York: Scholastic.

Terban, M. (2008). *The dove dove.* Boston: Houghton Mifflin.

Vander Ark, B. (1996). The freshman. On *Enemies* [CD]. New York: BMG.

Warburton, T. (Director). (2002). *Schoolhouse rock* [DVD]. New York: Walt Disney Video.

Wedge, C. (Director). (2002). *Ice age* [Film]. New York: 20th Century Fox.

Whedon, J. (Writer). (1997–2003). *Buffy the vampire slayer.* [Television series]. Beverly Hills, CA: Mutant Enemy Productions.

White, E. B. (1952). *Charlotte's web.* New York: HarperCollins.

Wise, R. (Director). (1951). *The day the earth stood still* [Film]. New York: 20th Century Fox.

References

Alvermann, D. (2001). Reading adolescents' reading identities: Looking back to see ahead. *Journal of Adolescent & Adult Literacy, 44*, 676–690.

Alvermann, D. E. (2008). Why bother theorizing adolescents' online literacies for classroom practice and research? *Journal of Adolescent & Adult Literacy, 52*, 8–19.

Alvermann, D. E., Hagood, M. C., Heron-Hruby, A., Hughes, P., Williams, K. B., & Yoon, J. (2007). Telling themselves who they are: What one out-of-school time study revealed about underachieving readers. *Reading Psychology, 28*, 1–19.

Alvermann, D. E., Moon, J. S., & Hagood, M. C. (1999). *Popular culture in the classroom: Teaching and researching critical media literacy.* Newark, DE: International Reading Association/National Reading Conference.

Beach, R., & O'Brien, D. (2008). Teaching popular culture texts in the classroom. In J. Coiro, M. Knobel, C. Lankshear, & D. J. Leu (Eds.), *Handbook of research on new literacies* (pp. 775–804). New York: Erlbaum/Taylor & Francis Group.

Black, R. W. (2005). Access & affiliation: The literacy and composition practices of English-language learners in an online fan fiction community. *Journal of Adolescent & Adult Literacy, 49*, 118–128.

Black, R. W. (2008). *Adolescents and online fan fiction.* New York: Peter Lang.

Boje, D. M. (2001). *Narrative methods for organizational and communication research.* Thousand Oaks, CA: Sage.

Bruce, D. L. (2008). Visualizing literacy: Building bridges with media. *Reading and Writing Quarterly, 24*, 264–282.

Buckingham, D. (2003). *Media education: Literacy, learning and contemporary culture.* Malden, MA: Polito Press.

Burmark, L. (2007). Visual literacy: What you get is what you see. In N. Frey & D. Fisher (Eds.), *Teaching visual literacy* (pp. 5–25). Thousand Oaks, CA: Corwin.

Burn, A. (2007). "Writing" computer games: Game literacy and new-old narratives. *L1 Educational Studies in Language and Literature, 7*(4), 45–67.

Carlson, D., & Apple, M. W. (1998). *Power/knowledge/pedagogy: The meaning of democratic education in unsettling times.* Boulder, CO: Westview.

Chandler, K. (2000). Rethinking the reading–writing workshop: Tensions and negotiations between a Stephen King reader and her teacher. *Reading Research and Instruction, 39*(2), 135–159.

Cohen, R. (1998). Tricks of the trade: On teaching arts and "race" in the classroom. In D. Buckingham (Ed.), *Teaching popular culture: Beyond radical pedagogy* (pp. 153–176). London: UCL Press.

Comber, B., & Kamler, B. (2005). *Turn-around pedagogies: Literacy interventions for at-risk students.* Sydney, Australia: Primary English Teaching Association.

Cowan, J. (2008). Diary of a blog: Listening to kids in an elementary school library. *Teacher Librarian, 35*(5), 20–26.

Dewey, J. (1916). *Democracy and education: An introduction to the philosophy of education.* New York: MacMillan.

Duff, P. A. (2004). Intertextuality and hybrid discourses: The infusion of pop culture in educational discourse. *Linguistics and Education, 14,* 231–276.

Faust, M. (2000). Reconstructing familiar metaphors: John Dewey and Louise Rosenblatt on literary art as experience. *Research in the Teaching of English, 35,* 9–34.

Fish, S. (1980). *Is there a text in this class?: The authority of interpretive communities.* Cambridge, MA: Harvard University Press.

Fisher, R., Harris, A., & Jarvis, C. (2008). *Education in popular culture: Telling tales on teachers and learners.* New York: Routledge.

Freire, P. (1973). *Pedagogy of the oppressed.* Hagerstown, MN: Harper & Row.

Friese, E. (2008). Popular culture in the school library: Enhancing literacies traditional and new. *School Libraries Worldwide, 14*(2). Retrieved March 1, 2009, from http://schoollibrariesworldwide-vol14no2.blogspot.com/

Funge, E. (1998). Rethinking representation: Media studies and the postmodern teenager. *English and Media Magazine, 39,* 33–36.

Gee, J. P. (1996). *Social linguistics and literacies: Ideology in discourse* (2nd ed.). London: Taylor & Francis.

Gee, J. P. (2003). *What video games have to teach us about learning and literacy.* New York: Palgrave Macmillan.

Guzzetti, B. (2009). Thinking like a forensic scientist: Learning with academic and everyday texts. *Journal of Adolescent & Adult Literacy, 53*(3), 192–203.

Hagood, M. C. (2002). Critical literacy for whom? *Reading Research and Instruction, 41*(3), 247–266.

Hagood, M. C. (2007). Linking popular culture to literacy learning and teaching in the 21st century. In B. Guzzetti (Ed.), *Literacy for the new millennium: Adolescent literacy* (Vol. 3), (pp. 223–238). Westport CT: Praeger.

Hagood, M. C. (2008). Intersections of popular culture, identities, and new literacies research. In J. Coiro, D. Leu, M. Knobel, & C. Lankshear (Eds.), *Handbook of research on new literacies* (pp. 531–551). New York: Peter Lang.

Hagood, M. C., Provost, M., Skinner, E., & Egelson, P. (2008). Teachers' and students' literacy performance in and engagement with new literacies strategies in underperforming middle schools. *Middle Grades Research Journal 3*, 57–95.

Hagood, M. C., Stevens, L. P., & Reinking, D. (2002). What do *they* have to teach *us*? Talkin' 'cross generations! In D. E. Alvermann (Ed.), *Adolescents and literacies in a digital world* (pp. 68–83). New York: Peter Lang.

Hill, M. L. (2009). *Beats, rhymes, and classroom life: Hip-hop pedagogy and the politics of identity*. New York: Teachers College Press.

Hobbs, R. (2007). *Reading the media: Media literacy in high school English*. New York: Teachers College Press.

Hogue, D. (2008, February). Blogs, wikis, & web 2.0 in the classroom. Paper presented at the Wisconsin State Reading Association. Retrieved June 28, 2009, from http://www.mshogue.com/wsra_08.htm

Hull, G., & Zacher, J. (2004, Winter/Spring). What is after-school worth? Developing literacy and identity out of school. *Voices in Urban Education*, pp. 36–44.

Irwin, J. (2006). *Teaching reading comprehension processes* (3rd ed.). Upper Saddle River, NJ: Allyn & Bacon.

Jabari, M. (2001). Pop culture pedagogy and the end(s) of school. *Journal of Adolescent & Adult Literacy, 44*, 382–385.

Jacobs, G. (2008). We learn what we do: Developing a repertoire of writing practices in an instant messaging world. *Journal of Adolescent & Adult Literacy, 52*, 203–213.

Jewitt, C. (2008). Multimodality and literacy in school classrooms. *Review of research in education, 32*(1), 241–267.

Jewitt, C., & Kress, G. (Eds.). (2003). *Multimodal literacy*. New York: Peter Lang.

Knobel, M. (1999). *Everyday literacies*. New York: Peter Lang.

Knobel, M., & Lankshear, C. (2007). Sampling "the new" in new literacies. In M. Knobel & C. Lankshear (Eds.), A new literacies sampler (pp. 1–24). New York: Peter Lang.

Kristeva, J. (1980). Word, dialogue, and novel (L. S. Roudiez, Trans.; T. Gora et al., Eds.). *Desire and language* (pp. 64–91). New York: Columbia University Press.

Lankshear, C., & Knobel, M. (2006). *New literacies: Everyday practices and classroom learning*. Berkshire, UK: Open University Press.

Lenhart, A., Madden, M., Macgill, A. R., & Smith, A. (2007, December). Teens and social media. *Pew Internet & American Life Project*. Washington, DC: Pew Charitable Trusts. Retrieved October 15, 2008, from www.pewinternet.org/PPF/r/230/report_display.asp

Marsh, J. (2008). Popular culture in the language arts classroom. In J. Flood, S. B. Heath, & D. Lapp (Eds.), *Handbook of research on teaching literacy through the communicative and visual arts* (Vol. II, pp. 529–536). New York: Erlbaum/Taylor & Francis Group.

McTaggart, J. (2008). Graphic novels: The good, the bad, and the ugly. In N. Frey & D. Fisher (Eds.), *Teaching visual literacy* (pp. 27–46). Thousand Oaks, CA: Corwin.

Millard, E. (2003). Toward a literacy of fusion: New times, new teachings and learning? *Reading, Literacy and Learning, 37*(1), 3–9.

Millard, E. (2006).Transformative pedagogy: Creating a literacy of fusion. In K. Pahl & J. Rowsell (Eds.), *Travel notes from the new literacy studies: Instances of practice* (pp. 234–253). Clevedon, UK: Multilingual Matters.

Morrell, E. (2008). *Critical literacy and urban youth: Pedagogies of access, dissent, and liberation.* New York: Routledge.

Morrell, E., & Duncan-Andrade, J. (2002). Promoting academic literacy with urban youth through engaging hip-hop culture. *English Journal, 91*(6), 88–92.

National Council of Teachers of English. (2008). *NCTE framework for 21st century curriculum and assessment.* Retrieved February 25, 2009, from http://www.ncte.org/library/NCTEFiles/Resources/Positions/Framework_21stCent_Curr_Assessment.pdf

Okan, Z. (2007). Edutainment: Is learning at risk? *British Journal of Educational Technology, 34*(3), 255–264.

Pahl, K., & Rowsell, J. (2006). *Travel notes from the New Literacy Studies: Instances of practice.* Buffalo, NY: Multilingual Matters.

Pahl, K., & Rowsell, J. (in press). *Artifactual literacy: Every object tells a story.* New York: Teachers College Press.

Pendergrass, E. (2008). Using pop-culture novels to promote engagement. *Signal: The Journal of the IRA Special Interest Group on Literature for the Adolescent Reader, 30*(2), 12–15.

Pryor, G. S. (2008). Using pop culture to teach introductory biology. *The American Biology Teacher, 70*(7), 396–399.

Sanford, K. (2008). Video games in the library? What is the world coming to? *School Libraries Worldwide, 14*(2), 83–88.

Short, K. G., & Kauffman, G. (2000). Exploring sign systems within an inquiry system. In M. A. Gallego & S. Hollingsworth (Eds.), *What counts as literacy: Challenging the school standard* (pp. 42–61). New York: Teachers College Press.

Shusterman, R. (2000). *Performing live: Aesthetic alternatives for the ends of art.* Ithaca, NY: Cornell University Press.

Skinner, E. (2007). Writing workshop meets critical media literacy: Using magazines and movies as mentor texts. *Voices from the Middle, 15*(2), 30–39.

Spires, H., Lee, J., Turner, K., & Johnson, J. (2008). Having our say: Middle grade student perspectives on school, technologies, and academic engagement. *Journal of Research in Technology on Education, 40*, 497-515.

Spiro, R. J., Coulson, R. L., Feltovich, P. J., & Anderson, D. (1988). Cognitive flexibility theory: Advanced knowledge acquisition in ill-structured domains. In V. Patel (Ed.), *Proceedings of the 10th annual conference of the Cognitive Science Society* (pp. 375–383). Hillsdale, NJ: Erlbaum.

Spiro, R. J., & Jehng, J. (1990). Cognitive flexibility and hypertext: Theory and technology for the nonlinear and multidimensional traversal of complex subject matter. In D. Nix & R. Spiro (Eds.), *Cognition, education, and multimedia: Exploring ideas in high technology* (pp. 163–205). Hillsdale, NJ: Erlbaum.

Squire, K. (2008). Video-game literacy: A literacy of expertise. In J. Coiro, M. Knobel, C. Lankshear, & D. J. Leu (Eds.), *The handbook of research on new literacies* (pp. 635–669). New York: Erlbaum/Taylor & Francis Group.

Stevens, L., & Bean, T. (2007). *Critical literacy: Content, research, and practice in K–12 classrooms.* Thousand Oaks, CA: Sage.

Street, B. V. (1995). *Social literacies.* New York: Addison Wesley.

Varga-Dobai, K. (2008). From folktales to popular culture: Poaching and relevance in the process of history. *Folklore* [online], *40*, 21–36. Retrieved March 1, 2009, from http://www.folklore.ee/folklore/vol40/varga.pdf

Vasudevan, L. M. (2006). Looking for Angels: Knowing adolescents by engaging with their multimodal literacy practices. *Journal of Adolescent & Adult Literacy, 50*, 252–256.

Venters, M. (2009). Day of tears/day of desperation: Using blogging to make social studies content engaging and comprehensible. In M. Hagood (Ed.), *New literacies practices: Designing literacy learning* (pp. 77–90). New York: Peter Lang.

Weinstein, S. (2006). A love for the thing: The pleasures of rap as a literate practice. *Journal of Adolescent & Adult Literacy, 50*, 270–281.

Xu, S. H. (2004). Teachers' reading of students' popular culture texts: The interplay of students' interests, teacher knowledge, and literacy curriculum. In J. Worthy, M. Maloch, J. V. Hoffman, D. L. Schallert, & C. M. Fairbanks (Eds.), *53rd yearbook of the National Reading Conference* (pp. 417–431). Oak Creek, WI: National Reading Conference.

Xu, S. H. (with R. S. Perkins & L. O. Zunich). (2005). *Trading cards to comic strips: Popular culture texts and literacy learning in grades K–8.* Newark, DE: International Reading Association.

Index

Academic literacies, 29
Adamson, A., 34, 83
After-school program, 72
Alcatraz Versus the Evil Librarians (Sanderson), 76, 84
Alcott, L. M., 6, 83
Alvermann, D. E., x, 14, 18, 30, 38, 56, 63, 72, 85, 87, 98
American Revolution, 32
Anderson, D., 43, 54, 83, 88
Anderson, M. T., 43, 83
Angelou, M., 38, 83
Animé, 2, 23, 29, 44, 79, 81
"Another Brick in the Wall: Part I" (Pink Floyd), 54, 84
Apple, M. W., 39, 86
Artifacts, 4, 15, 17, 50, 74, 79
Assessments, 27
Audiences, 2, 9, 11, 14, 15, 20, 27, 30, 36, 37, 39, 41, 44, 59, 60, 61, 80–82
multiple, 37
peer, 43
Authorial intent, 3, 61, 62

Barrett-Jones, L., 70, 71, 75, 76, 78
Bass, R., 63, 83
Beach, R., 76, 77, 85
Bean, T., 4, 30, 89
Beats, Rhymes, and Classroom Life (Hill), 40, 87
Beecroft, S., 21, 83
Belief systems, 2, 11
Black, R. W., 44, 45, 85
Blog/blogging, 3, 4, 13, 15,

20-23, 25, 29, 41, 74, 75, 79, 86, 87, 89
Boje, D. M., 21, 85
Brooks, G., 6, 83
Brown, C., 48, 56
Brown, N., 8
Bruce, D. L., 28, 85
Bryant, M., 39, 40, 41
Buckingham, D., 56, 57, 85, 86
Buffy the Vampire Slayer (TV show), 44, 84
Bullying, 31, 40, 41, 68
Burmark, L., 44, 85
Burn, A., 18, 44, 45, 86

Campbell, T., 51
Canon, 36, 37, 41, 43
Carlson, D., 39, 86
Cartoons, 15, 29, 38, 44, 81
Cell phone, 15, 32, 73, 77
Censorship, 23
Chandler, K., 2, 5, 24, 86
Charlotte's Web (White), 20, 83, 84
Civil War, 6, 29
Clark, R., 73
Cobain, K., 56, 61, 83
Cohen, R., 68, 86
Collective action, 72
Collier, N., 13, 14, 17
Comber, B., 71, 74, 75, 77, 82, 86
Community of trust, 63, 64
Composition, 28, 33, 44, 85
Comprehension, 27, 32, 38, 40, 46, 87
Cooper, T., 48, 49, 56, 76
Coulson, R., 54, 88

Cowan, J., 14, 21, 22, 23, 75, 86
Critical awareness, 30, 37, 79
Critical consciousness, 37, 79
Critical framing, in literacy, 57, 79
Critical literacy, 86, 88, 89
Critical model, for literacy instruction, 29, 30, 44
Critique, 28, 29, 77
Cross, C., 61, 83
The Crow and the Pitcher (Aesop), 78
CSI (TV show), 39, 65, 83
Cultural capital model, for literacy instruction, 29, 30
Cultural resources, 35
Culture
everyday, 9–11, 14, 15, 18, 27, 29–31, 52, 56, 59, 60, 62, 73, 80, 82
school, 76
Curricular concepts, 18

Dabit, C., 2, 26, 31–34, 35, 75
Dangerous Minds (film), 63, 83
The Day the Earth Stood Still (film), 55, 84
De La Cruz, M., 43, 83
Dem Heizman Boyz, 60, 83
Dewey, J., 56, 86
Direct instruction, 40, 51
Donahue, A., 39, 83
The Dove Dove (Terban), 78, 84
Duff, P. A., 18, 86
Duncan-Andrade, J., 18, 29, 88

About the Authors

Margaret C. Hagood teaches courses in 21st-century literacies, including pop culture, at the College of Charleston in the department of teacher education. Margaret has taught late elementary grades and middle grades in Washington, D.C., and Georgia. She's a big fan of Michael Franti and Spearhead, mixed music burns and mashups, and YouTube.

Donna E. Alvermann teaches courses in popular culture and adolescent literacy at the University of Georgia, where she holds the title of Distinguished Research Professor in Language and Literacy Education. Donna has been a middle/junior high school teacher in Houston, Texas, and Elmira, New York. She has been a fan of "all things pop culture" since the mid-1950s, when she was president of the James Dean Fan Club. Currently, she counts Facebook, YouTube, and Second Life among her favorite pop culture texts.

Alison Heron-Hruby teaches English methods courses at George Mason University, where she is an assistant professor of English education. She also taught middle school and high school English, first on Long Island and then in Atlanta, Georgia. She has two young daughters—Katie and Evelyn—and a cat named Max. Her favorite pop culture texts include *People* magazine, Avril Lavigne's music, and the television show *Mad Men*.